BEYOND THE AFFAIR
The Healing of a Marriage

D1264898

Cover design by j. Gregory Barton, BrittBarton.com, Washington, DC.
Cover photo by Ken Kinnett.

Manufactured in the United States of America.
2001

Publisher:
Booklocker.com, Inc.
P.O. Box 2399
Bangor, ME 04402, USA
Fax 207-262-9696
http://www.booklocker.com

Library of Congress Card Number 2001117069

BEYOND THE AFFAIR

The Healing of a Marriage

LOYD KINNETT

Take heart!
Loyd Kinnett
8.18.2016

BEYOND THE AFFAIR
The Healing of a Marriage

DEDICATION

This book is dedicated to the healing of humankind on
"...this fragile earth, our island home."
May we recognize and know
we are one.

Table of Contents

Part I, The Caterpillar, focuses on survival. Just as a caterpillar spends its days looking for food to survive, Loyd's days are focused on how she can survive with or without Ken. Always lurking in the background is the question of whether the marriage will survive.

Part II, The Chrysalis, is the "in-between-place" where change is beginning to occur in Loyd and Ken's life together. Sometimes it was as though nothing had changed at all, and then a breakthrough moment of profound truth would appear with new possibilities on the horizon.

BEYOND THE AFFAIR

PART III: THE BUTTERFLY 124
    Part III, The Butterfly, is the emerging of new awareness born out of betrayal, suffering, and the hard labor it takes for transformation to occur. The final chapters speak of the real meaning of forgiveness and commitment. Loyd and Ken meet with Jane, and Ken's Afterword leaves no doubt that marriages can heal after the trauma of an affair.

Preface

When betrayal shatters a relationship, it can be difficult to mend it. *Beyond the Affair: The Healing of a Marriage* is the story of how my husband and I were able to preserve, and even strengthen, our marriage of thirty-nine years following his affair. Some of this difficult work was done together, with guidance from a wise counselor and loving friends and family, but in great measure the task of deciding to stay in the marriage, to forgive and move forward, fell on my shoulders. How this journey unfolded for me is the focus of this book.

Everyone who is mentioned in the book graciously gave me permission to use his or her name. "Jane" is an exception. I did not use her real name to honor her anonymity. She could be anyone. You may have had your own similar experience, and can substitute another name in your mind as you read.

Whenever I am searching for answers in a particular book, I immediately go to the contents page and run my eye down the names of the chapters looking for the key words which will solve my quandary. There is no one chapter in *Beyond the Affair* that has the magic solution. Instead, the unfolding of the story will give you what you are wanting. To that end, do your best not to chapter hop and simply begin at the beginning with Chapter 1.

The book begins with my journal. All my journal entries are written in *italics* throughout the book.

Acknowledgments

As I think of acknowledging everyone who helped me write this book and those who were also with me as I lived through the affair, a picture comes into my mind. I see an excited, proud, nervous actress clutching an Oscar to her breast. She plunges in thanking everyone she ever knew for fear she would leave someone out. So it is with me! I too want to acknowledge everyone, and that could turn into a sizable book. However, I will move ahead trusting I will remember everyone who kept loving me forward.

With a grateful heart filled with love and admiration, I give thanks for my beloved Ken. His solid stance and belief in my writing this book created a safe and unwavering place for me to write whatever I thought needed to be said. He truly cheered me on, often through his own tears of remembering the hurt and pain I experienced.

Brian, David, and Annie—our amazing children—your continual support for me throughout this process, and for your dad as well, speaks volumes to me of your compassion and your capacity to love. I am a proud mama.

To my friends—thank you, thank you:

Rebecca Poole—for your frequent challenges, "You've got to write a book," and for holding on to me when I was in pain. Debbie Weber—for your ability to see when I couldn't and loving me through it all. June Krug—for your steadfast love of me that has withstood time and distance. John Hoover—for your patience and willingness to trust me. Michael Owens—for lovingly challenging us. Cynthia Schwenk—for your consistency and total lack of judging me or Ken. David Templer—for being one of the first to plant the seed that there was a book to be written. The co-founders of The Life Training, Brad Brown and Roy Whitten, as well as Sue Oldham and all the trainers—for being my mentors, teachers, and friends. Through the many Life Training courses my family and I experienced, I learned to appreciate the gifts life has to offer. Carolyn Cummings—for your gift of touching into the heart of my guides and generously sharing the good news. Nancy Zimmers, my business coach and friend—for encouraging me to have fun and do it my way. "The T-Girls"—Joy Drake, Kathy Tyler, Sallie Lee, Diana McKendree, and Nancy Zimmers—for our monthly gatherings that give me feedback, things to ponder, laughs, tears, which all enliven and transform my life. Dear Diana—for your willingness to read and reread, take apart, put back together, generally work with me and my book, you have been a godsend. Judy King of Judy King Editorial Services—for being the first to put a professional eye on my first few pages and responding with gusto. Susan Snowden—who edited and encouraged and gets excited every time she speaks of the book. The Western North Carolina Writers' Guild—a group of peers who are willing to share their knowledge and continually challenge me to persevere. Greg Barton—I will be forever grateful for your energy, loving heart, and belief in me. Your company, BrittBarton, has as part of its logo "Ignite your vision" and, thanks to you, my vision has never been brighter. Again, thank you all.

Introduction

This book may come as a surprise to some of our friends and relatives. It has taken courage for me to sit down and write it and enormous courage for Ken to support me and urge me on. Surprise or not, its time has come. What is in this book needs to be said—not just for healing on my part (although that is enough of a reason to write) but also for those of you, men and women, who sit with the pain of what you think you know, afraid to uncover your spouse's love affair. Or perhaps the affair has been uncovered and you have decided to stay together, manage, carry on, with everything changed and nothing changed, wanting it to be different but afraid it will always be the way it is now, hopeless.

I know that fear.

I also know there is another way you can live your life other than sit with your pain and fear. It takes work, furious work! You can move forward even though you have believed change isn't within your reach.

This is a book of hope, hope for those who *want* to have a relationship but believe it has been completely broken by an affair. You may be right; then again, you may find the affair to be an opportunity, an opportunity that would not have come along without the affair. New possibilities are within your reach. Working together, you can have everything either one of you ever wanted.

PART I: THE CATERPILLAR

1.

Voicing the Pain

It's 2 a.m. I am so tired. I feel used, dirty, crazy. I don't want to leave my home, my dogs, my friends, my husband. Touching Ken today was so painful. I love the way he feels and smells. There is a huge "but" in here. But if he doesn't love me, what does it matter how much I love to touch him—what does any of it matter?

We have worked together for years and he thinks we could still work together, be friends, I can't believe this! He is having an affair with Jane, is thinking of leaving me, wants to continue to work with me, be my friend—what's wrong with this picture? I don't even know what I want! I do know I want this stuff to disappear. I want a husband who will love me, cherish me. I want him to be Ken. Where is Ken? The years and years I lived with his depression, worked with him, cared for him, cherished him. No guarantees, no guarantees.

Jane, of all people. I thought she was a friend. I am confused and hurt. It is so hard to believe she is sleeping with Ken.

Fury shakes my body as I write. I have been yelling everything that was on my heart. The knowledge of how betrayed and unloved I feel fills the air. I cried, screamed, sobbed, swore. As soon as I thought I could cry no more, up would bubble more fury.

My body rocks back and forth on the sofa as I beat myself up with all the wild questions that fill my head. All this must be my fault. What have I done to create this? Did I tell him too much about how I was feeling sexually? Did he take my menopausal struggle as some kind of reflection of his sex appeal, or

16

lack of appeal? Have I taken him for granted? Did I not tell him how much I love him?

In my quiet moments I can hear the neighbor's dog barking in the distance. Normally, Taylor keeps us awake and is a middle-of-the-night nuisance. Tonight I feel his companionship—barking and howling since 10 p.m. I think perhaps he is doing this for me. Bark and howl, dog; bark and howl, bark and howl.

For the first time in my life, the thought has come to me that death would be a great relief. I've been sitting here looking at the stairway leading up to the second floor of the cabin. The risers are open, and from this angle I see how easy it would be to tie my bathrobe sash around the step and my neck and jump. No more pain, no more worrying if he loved me, no more concerns if he was 95 percent ready to leave me, no thinking about who the next woman might be— no more.

I sit in a boat of lies in a lake of lies. Oh, God, what do I do? No more barking dog.

The morning of my discovery began.

I was wide awake. Rolling over, I saw the radio clock glowing 5:30. It was not like me to be so wide awake at such an early hour. What woke me? Ken was sleeping peacefully, breathing deeply, facing me with the relaxed sealed-eye sleep of the undisturbed. I could feel Dickens, our oldest Jack Russell terrier, in his favorite sleeping place curled up against my side, still. I felt around with my feet for Dickens's sister, Clio. No Clio. She was probably on the pillow of the big chair in the corner of the bedroom.

Lying in the warmth of our bed, I became aware of a sinking feeling bordering on anxiety, creepy, uneasy, deep in the pit of me. I looked again at Ken. Sometimes when he is depressed, I can feel his anxiety or some inner fearfulness that transmits from him to me. Usually it is when he is right up next to me holding me. He doesn't look depressed and he isn't up next to me. Odd.

BEYOND THE AFFAIR

As I wrote this last paragraph four years after the event, Clio began throwing up at my feet. Amazing. I can't help but think how incredibly appropriate. I was beginning to write down the most painful time of my life, and my dog throws up at my feet. I don't believe in accidents. She was demonstrating just exactly how I was feeling. Thank you, dear dog, for your gift of connectedness.

Looking back is wonderful. When I was in the midst of discovering and later in such pain, I would have given anything to look back on what was going on, mainly because it would all be over and, hopefully, there would be no more pain.

There are moments of truth in our lives when everything changes. For me it was soon after that 5:30 a.m. wake-up. Sitting on the window seat at the breakfast room table waiting for Ken to come home from, of all things, a Rotary Club meeting, I knew. I knew why I was feeling so anxious, so fearful. Almost forty years into our marriage, Ken was having an affair.

It makes no difference how I found out or what the gory details are. (We have certainly been fed enough "affair details" from the Clinton/Lewinsky episode for me to decline to add mine.) It doesn't even matter who the "other" woman was. What does make a difference is what happened next. What did I do; what did he do? How did I/we get beyond the affair?

The feelings and process we went through are similar to the healing any couple must face to restore a shattered marriage. The issues we had may not be a perfect match with yours, but the pain and the opportunity to learn and rethink your life together will be a part of any rebuilding effort. Effort it certainly was, but well worth it all. Your pain can bring new hope to your life also.

The confrontation that afternoon in our kitchen was incredibly painful. As I heard Ken's car drive up the driveway, I prayed, "Please don't make me right. You know I love to be right, but not now, not in this case."

The car door slammed, the downstairs door opened, and he called out as he came up the stairs, "I'm home."

I was terrified. As he put his briefcase on the table, I said, "Something is wrong. Something is very wrong."

His face turned white and he looked as frightened as I felt. Then I asked the big question I had prayed would not be answered the way I had feared, "Are you having an affair?"

Silence.

"Yes."

Sitting there on the window seat, I could feel the blood leave my face, and I thought for a moment I was going to faint. I felt absolutely nothing. No fear, no anger, nothing. I do not remember what was said next. Perhaps I asked who or maybe I said something about not believing it was true. Whatever. I was totally stunned, shocked. I really could not believe this was happening to me, to us.

Here in the comfort of my own kitchen I felt I was transported to some other planet and I had no clue as to why we were in such an incredible dilemma. I began to listen to the incomprehensible words coming out of Ken's mouth.

"I am 95 percent sure I am going to leave you," he stated flatly.

"You are what?"

"I am pretty sure I am ready to leave you. I think forty years is time enough."

Stuttering and trying to find the words, I stammered, "You make it sound like a prison sentence. You've done your time!"

"Something like that. I have no sexual feelings for you anymore. I feel ambivalent. Two weeks ago I stopped the sexual relationship with Jane because I want to make a clear decision."

"Jane? You're having an affair with Jane? I can't believe you are saying this."

19

BEYOND THE AFFAIR

I was astonished. Jane and I have been in each other's homes, worked on a project together, and all the while I worked so hard to help her excel in what she wanted to do. Though unmarried, I had no idea she had any interest in Ken, other than a friend, much less Ken wanting her interest.

We talked back and forth. I was trying to make sense of what he was saying, and Ken was trying to make sense of it to me and maybe to himself too. But there we were—he was ready to leave and I was reeling from the sudden turn in my life. Both of us were in enormous pain.

The hurt soon began to pour over me and with tears streaming down my cheeks I began to ask, "How could you do this to me, to us? I thought we loved each other and were committed to each other. We have worked so hard on our relationship. This makes no sense to me. How could you?"

Silence.

"Why couldn't you talk to me about all this? What could you be thinking? How could you not love me? Am I so sexually unattractive to you that you had to find somebody else?"

"You aren't unattractive. I do love you, but not the way I used to."

Nothing he said made any sense to me. We had always told each other everything. He was my best friend, my confidant, my heart of hearts. How could he be saying these things to me? I had trusted him, encouraged him, moved from career to career with him, and look where we were now.

For years we considered our relationship to be great and one of the most important things in our lives. We were often struck by how special our relationship was when we encountered other people who were having such a miserable time together. Workshops on personal growth were something we enjoyed together. We even moved ten years ago from a large city to a small town in western North Carolina believing it would add years to our lives and certainly to our marriage.

It had become clear that as hard as we had worked on our relationship, we had not automatically been rewarded with the exceptional marriage I thought we had.

2.

Rallying the Troops

As I answered the phone, I knew there was no keeping secret the earlier events of the day. Holding my tears back, I managed, "Hello."

On the line was a friend Ken and I worked with who had a regularly scheduled phone call with us. Sue Oldham was our contact with a nonprofit educational foundation we had been working with for a number of years. She was more than a contact. She had become a caring friend, who knew our ups and downs, challenged us to move forward with our vision of how we wanted to work with the foundation, and had the ability to cut through the garbage and tell the truth. We counted on her for her truth telling and she counted on ours.

Ken joined me on the speaker phone. As Sue heard us pour out the events of the last few hours, she listened with an open heart—helping us do the same. "Loyd," she said, "this is your worst nightmare." That was the truth! "I can hear the pain in both of your voices. It looks like you are in a quandary, Ken, and don't know what you want to do." The truth again.

More was said about the inner work we both needed to do. She gave lots of loving support to the both of us—no "advice," no trying to fix it, but a clear trust in us that somehow made the moment a slight bit lighter. Unfortunately, it was only a moment.

Sue was one voice of many who reached out to be with us during our ordeal. I am amazed at what good care we took of ourselves those first few months. The very first day without thinking about it, we began to rally support around ourselves.

The first call we made was to our therapist, John Hoover, whose office is two and a half hours away. The receptionist told us he was many more miles away in Costa Rica and wouldn't return for two weeks. Though we didn't see him regularly, both of us knew he could help us whether Ken stayed in our marriage or left. Off and on we have seen a therapist when we have wanted to work through issues we have had in relating to one another and have benefited from what we learned.

I panicked! Two weeks without John felt like a death sentence. Searching for what else we could do, we realized we could go to Michael, a friend who was also an Episcopal priest like Ken. We believed he could help us and made an appointment the very next day. Both of us have worked through enough crises in our lives to know we didn't need to be alone with our struggle.

We also called our children. It is fortunate to be in a place in life where your children have become your best friends. I wanted to talk with them, share where we were, hear what they had to say. Mostly I wanted the comfort of hearing their voices and feeling their love. I knew whatever happened between Ken and me, they would love me.

I was not prepared for the warmth of their response, and I was so proud of them. As their parents, I think we have done an exceptional job. Each in his own way listened to us without rushing into judging. It would have been so easy to let their hurt and anger take over. Instead they voiced their dismay about what had happened.

Neither Brian nor Annie was particularly surprised by the affair, only the way Ken went about it. They thought he had expressed interest in other women before. Ken had often voiced to me that in his mind he had not had time to "sow his wild oats" or some such hooey since we had married at such an early age (eighteen and twenty-one) and he had soon afterwards become an Episcopal priest. The children thought if their dad had wanted to have other relationships, he could simply have asked for a divorce. That way he would still be in integrity with himself and me, their mom. Sure sounded better than sneaking behind my

23

back and having an affair. All of us were having problems with Ken's humanity—even Ken.

It was especially hard for our son David. Annie and Brian were living in Atlanta and kept in close touch. David was in Colorado. Ken's behavior destroyed David's idealistic view of the wonderful relationship his parents had—not that this was a bad thing. Brian and Annie weren't quite as convinced of how perfect we were. It just took David longer to give up his idealized picture of us, and it was painful to hear his struggle.

3.

The Dark of Night

Nighttime came and Ken offered to leave if I needed to be alone. I said no. Truthfully, I was afraid to be alone and afraid he would go to Jane. It was an evening and night of hell. I don't remember eating or talking. I do remember the moment of going to bed. How awkward. After thirty-nine years of crawling into the same bed with Ken, I felt lost, unwanted, undesirable, unloved.

There is very little that can keep Ken awake when it is time to go to sleep. This night was no different. The dogs piled into bed with him, and I retreated to the cabin part of the house, feigning I was too wide awake to go to sleep now. That was a lie; I felt exhausted, but I didn't want to be somewhere I wasn't wanted.

There are many beautiful things about our home. First, it is a charming log cabin that sits on top of a mountain. The views stretch forever, particularly in the winter when the leaves are off the trees. The cabin was originally designed for weekend visits only. There were no closets, no attic, no basement, and a tiny difficult-to-work-in kitchen. So we built an addition that gave us much needed space—a bedroom with real closets, a kitchen (with the infamous window seat and kitchen table) with plenty of room in the pantry and lots of work space.

It was with comfort that I could go into the cabin that first night. Comfort because I could close the door between the old part and the new part of the house. I could cry and rant and rave and not worry about being heard.

The logs of the cabin are golden and with the light from the lamp by the sofa were welcoming. I needed to feel welcomed. Although the cabin isn't old by cabin standards, it still has a warmth and quality of age, wisdom, healing, and what I was looking for, comfort.

I am not imagining this "feel" about the cabin; we hear it from everyone who spends time here. Ken and I wanted this space to have healing transformational energy and named the cabin Mariposa, Spanish for "butterfly." We wanted people to come as caterpillars, cocoon in this wonderful space, and leave as butterflies.

That dreadful night I was definitely a caterpillar.

4.

Dawn

At one point today I was in so much pain I thought, at least Ken isn't dead—but I think this must feel worse. He has no romantic or sexual feelings for me. He feels ambivalent. I have no idea how long he has felt this way. Jane is in love with him and wants him to decide between us. Is he "in love" with her?

I feel so old and unloved—soon to be discarded like a worn-out shoe.

He says he wants to make a clear decision. What in the world does that mean? How do you decide between a new budding romance and an old unromantic, nonsexual relationship? Looks like a no-brainer to me. I can't believe this!!!

Dawn came quickly. Time flies when you're *not* having fun too. I had been hard at work. At my feet were piles of used tissue. My journal lay open in my lap. There were no sounds to be heard from Taylor, no barking, no howling. It was as though I had taken the cue from him and was quiet myself.

I looked over at the school-room clock, its chiming long quieted by old age. It was 7:15 a.m. I mused, "What a funny clock, unable to keep time unless it is slightly askew." Strangely, if the clock was straightened like it was a picture on the wall, it seemed to take offense and would stop ticking.

Tears began to flow again as I thought about how in the world we would take our home apart. Who would take what? It was all ours. What belonged to him? What belonged to me? What mysterious ways our minds wrap around the most innocuous things in the midst of pain. I was attached to minutiae as though decisions had to be made right then about everything. Everything that entered into my thinking seemed to be incredibly important and impossible to resolve.

I got up from the sofa feeling utterly exhausted. My legs were automatically moving me forward, but my body felt detached. Weak and spaghetti-legged, I managed to get to the kitchen sink. I poured cold well water into my cup thinking how good a cup of tea would taste.

"Are you all right?" Ken asked.

Startled, I turned around. I hadn't heard Ken come into the room. He looked sleepy and anxious as he came toward me. He had only his pajama top on and his bare feet appeared cold on the wooden floor.

"I was getting some tea."

"I thought you were throwing up in the sink."

Confused, I realized I had been sobbing, heaving sobs which seemed to have a life of their own. I hadn't heard myself.

Tea in hand, I started walking toward the cabin. With the naturalness of our long life together, Ken put his arm around me and guided me in the direction I wanted to go. He joined me as I sat down on the sofa. We talked and talked and cried and cried, just like the best friends we are. I shared the struggle of the night, and he marveled that I was so upset. He kept saying, "I had no idea this would be so painful for you."

Such an amazing statement. He didn't know that I would be so upset? How have we gotten so far apart? He had no clue I would be so crushed, devastated—none of these words quite fit. Nothing sounds strong enough to express the overpowering pain. Again I was back into the "nothing makes sense" stage of awareness.

5.

Buddha Dog

I have no idea how long we talked in the living room. At some point, Dickens made his presence known.

We called Dickens our Buddha dog as he was amazingly wise and "enlightened." There have been times I have been convinced he could read our minds. His death last year left a great hole in our hearts. He developed a brain tumor. When it began to be clear he could no longer enjoy nor care for himself, we had our vet put him down. Such grief we felt. Telling it now brings a lump into my throat and tears into my eyes.

The comfort this dog gave us through our crisis was a gift beyond anything we could ever have expected from anyone, let alone a dog! He loved us when we didn't love each other. He gave us his love unconditionally and made it so visible that we were taught in the process. You were blessed to have him curl up next to you. (Some of our non-doggie-lover friends only noticed the hair he left on their clothes, unaware of what had really transpired.) His paw resting on your leg and eyes looking up into your eyes redeemed any moment of pain.

Dickens was ready to go outside. We were taking serious liberty with his routine. It was very apparent that the household was in crisis. Both Dickens and Clio were totally intolerant of raised voices or tones that sound disrespectful, and especially loud sobs—quiet sobs were admissible.

Both Clio and Dickens were at the carport door, ready. With Dickens's leash in hand, Ken opened the door to let out Clio, who doesn't need to be leashed. With a great burst Dickens pushed Clio aside and out the door he flew.

In a matter of seconds Dickens could totally disappear without a trace. And when he was gone, he was long gone. Several times we thought we had lost him. We have had long hours of hunting the mountain for him, taking turns driving the car, calling for him, hours standing at the window watching the driveway for him to round the corner and sheepishly walk up the steps. This morning was not the time to be looking for a lost dog!

We waited a bit for Dickens to appear, but no such luck. Often when Dickens heard the car, he would come running for the thrill of a ride, but Ken, circling the mountain in his car, got no response this time. The only thing left to do was to wait it out or start walking and searching possible spots where Dickens might be.

Knowing there are no accidents, I realized that Dickens's great escape was his response to the chaos going on in his home. He was acting out what Ken and I wanted to do—make a dash for freedom from all this mess. Looking back, I believe that Dickens, in his great escape, was offering us an opportunity to completely change the direction in which we appeared to be going. Buddha dog was out to save us from making a huge mistake!

6.

The Cave

Dickens had been gone for hours. It was time to start walking. Of all the spots in which to look for Dickens first, Ken chose the Indian Cave.

The cave sits on our property just a short walk from the house. Located on the side of the mountain, it faces southwest. Many years ago it was used by the Cherokees as a place to hold rituals and store food. A sacred place.

Recently there was an old photo of the cave in the newspaper. It was taken in 1915. The women were dressed in long dresses, the men in starched collars picnicking among the rocks. Sometime in the '50s or '60s, the owner of the land became alarmed that children might get hurt playing in the cave and dynamited the entrance way. The cave no longer looks like a cave or what I think a cave should look like. It is more like a pile of interesting large rocks with an enormous overhang of granite. Such a tragedy. We have often thought of removing the huge stone that fell and fractured in front of the entrance.

Whether it looks like a cave or not, there is no doubt that the ground and space all around the cave are holy. You can feel the energy as you start down the side of the mountain. There is a pull as you come nearer to the entrance. Crawling up and sitting on the highest rock, you are face to face with a magnificent view. Looking out onto that beautiful piece of the world makes it easy to be still and quiet. Even though it is a "Be Not Afraid" space, the sense of many others looking out at the view with you can send shivers up your spine.

Approaching the cave from the west, Ken said he was worrying about making a decision to stay in the relationship or to go. Walking down toward the cave, he grasped a small sapling for support and, in that moment, his hand became one with the tree and the tree became as firm as an iron rod. There was no letting go—and he knew the answer to his quandary. There was no letting go. He would stay and work toward healing our marriage.

And, of course, guess who was sitting on the rocks waiting? Yes, Dickens, the Buddha dog.

7.

The Decision

Placing the leash securely on Dickens's collar, Ken began the walk back up the mountain. A walk filled with accusations. "You can't make such a decision so quickly. You are just trying to make it easy on yourself. You don't really mean it." He remembered something David Dean, a friend from the insurance business, had said, "You can turn failure into success in a second." Confident that his decision was solid, he continued the walk home.

The mind is an incredible thing. Just as my mind was racing with fear, so was Ken's. Bent on "being helpful," his mind was offering him every possibility ad nauseum and every scenario—all in stereophonic sound. This is the part of our mind that thinks it knows everything and is full of criticism. It also vehemently believes we need to be protected from the unknown.

I say "unknown" for the simple reason Ken had no idea how I would respond to his decision—or how the children or our friends would respond. Whether I'd laugh or throw my arms around him was unknown to him.

All of us constantly play the old "Fiddler on the Roof"—on the one hand, on the other hand. I want to make sure I do the right thing, say the right thing—in other words, be in control. I don't think I am alone in this. It is just that I/we forget that in reality we aren't in control of much of anything!

Once back home Ken eagerly shared his experience at the cave and his decision.

I listened with my heart beating hard.

BEYOND THE AFFAIR

"Will you take me back?" he asked.

With tears pouring down my face, I said, "Ken, I never sent you away."

Holding me, he said, "I realized I don't want to leave this place, the house, the dogs. I would be a fool to give all this up. I am willing to do whatever it takes—to hear your anger and your sadness. I want no more secrets either. There is nothing you can say to me I haven't told myself over and over again. I am so sorry and I do love you. I will bear all the pain I have caused you and all the pain you need to share with me."

I would like to say that, with a sigh of relief, all was forgiven and life went back to normal. But sitting at the breakfast room table, still in my pajamas, I was full of doubt. I heard our daughter Annie's voice on the phone from last night's conversation saying, "Mom, this is your opportunity to step into your power and go for what you want." Clueless at the time she said it, I began to have an inkling of what she meant.

8.

Affair Territory

We are meeting this afternoon with our friend Michael.

Ken came back from finding Dickens to tell me he had decided to be with me, stay in our marriage, if I will have him back. I never sent him away! We have some major work to do here. I cannot live with all the lies. When would I know what is true? There is no knowing. I don't know what to do. Maybe something will come out of our time with Michael, perhaps a plan.

In the meantime I am going to keep getting out all the pain I can. I am so full of anger. I don't even recognize myself. I could kill him. I don't know what I want. Not true. I want a husband who will cherish me and be faithful to me. And I don't think I have that right now.

I am too important to just take Ken back into my life. What does he want? It sounds more like he doesn't want to give up his home, this place, the cave, the view, his dogs. It doesn't sound like he wants me, all of me, me without house or dogs.

What is he willing to do? He has lied for months. I don't want the life we had; it is dead. There has been a tremendous rupture. I thought we were both living in honesty, truth, respect, kindness. It is an excruciatingly hard realization that all is a lie. What I believed to be true wasn't.

I want to say, and I will say, "You want me? You woo me! You start all over with me. You be present. Give of yourself for a change because all I have been getting is someone going through the motions—a robot. All I am getting is heartache."

BEYOND THE AFFAIR

When you leave our home, Mariposa, and travel down the mountain, the road is flanked by stands of rhododendron—some as tall as large trees. Zigzagging around the curves, it is easy to believe the legend that Solomon Jones, who long ago made most of the roads in this area, really did follow a cow down the mountain and created the road in its tracks.

Once arriving at the bottomland, you are treated to horses grazing in their pastures, small herds of cattle, rows of corn, and neat farm houses. You also get splendid views of these beautiful western North Carolina mountains. My heart leaps and I feel warm deep inside when I see the rolling ridges and the smooth curving lines of the blue gray mountains. There is a sensuousness to these old mountains, worn by the years—soft, feminine, and healing.

There are no megafarms in our area, just humble homes and farms of hardworking folks doing their best to make their living on the land. Living according to the whims of Mother Nature's son, El Niño, is not an easy life. Driving this road, I often feel grateful for and appreciative of the farmers' dedication and tenacity. "Bless them with bounty," I pray.

I had always enjoyed the forty-five minute drive to Asheville. I usually go the back roads to the interstate and on to Asheville. Though it is a narrow two-lane road, I miss the traffic of our town and am reminded of the beauty of the land. It is much more refreshing to the soul than driving by the mall and every food franchise there is.

Now everything had changed. Driving to Asheville to meet with Michael meant going into "affair territory." This was the place where secret trysts were held. Here were held the romantic meetings of two star-struck lovers living in their own little world—self-absorbed and bent on ignoring the possible pain their coupling could cause others. This was where plans and plottings were made as to when the next passionate meeting could be, how they would handle being around me and not give away their secret, when they could freely talk on the phone, where I would be so they could have their time together.

Here it is four years later and I sweat and feel the knot in my stomach as I write.

Secrets and the adventure of exploring a new love are such a potent aphrodisiac. Jane and Ken were masterful at their deception while I was trusting them both.

I felt sick and fearful the closer we got to Asheville. What was I afraid of? Was she going to pop up like a "jack in the box"? Was she going to confront me screaming in my face? Was she going to demand to have him back? Was she going to flaunt her sexual prowess, her ability to seduce my husband?

What was so frightening?

Was Ken going to use our time with Michael to recite all his unhappiness with me? Was he waiting to tell me he was really leaving after all? Did he just plain hate me? Was he going to seek revenge for my not being who he wanted me to be? Was he going to embarrass me and somehow expose me?

I was too deep into my fear to be able to name it. Instead I was swimming in a sea of anything and everything I thought it might be—working desperately hard to keep my head above water.

It took weeks to realize what I was fearing. Each time we drove to Asheville, I was afraid Ken was experiencing the drive as bringing him closer and closer to her. I was sure the memories of their meetings would be more than he could handle and he would change his mind. He would indeed move from 95 percent to 100 percent.

The fear of Ken running back into her arms stayed with me for a very long time. Actually, it was a revisited fear. Off and on in our marriage, I feared Ken would leave me. It wasn't an overt threat, but it was covert in behavior on the part of both of us. Hadn't he said to me on numerous occasions he hadn't sowed his wild oats? And hadn't I at times turned cold, unconsciously believing it was a way to punish him?

BEYOND THE AFFAIR

No one ever said to me learning to live in relationship would be easy or hard. Of course, having read every fairy tale I could feast my eyes on, I thought couples just lived happily ever after. This princess, however, had more than a pea hidden under her mattress keeping her awake at night.

I was obviously face to face with my worst fears. At this point in the journey, I wasn't in a place of being able to say, "Well, to hell with it. If Ken wants to flee to her arms and not rest in mine, then it is obvious he isn't really interested in doing anything with our relationship." Clear-headed Annie declared, "Mom, if you are afraid he will run to her, let him! If that's what he wants I wouldn't want him anyway." Easy to say, but hard to do when you love someone.

9.

Keep Him on the Griddle

With fear and trembling we arrived at our first appointment with Michael. Both of us were feeling very anxious. The possibility of our friendship with him changing was a part of our worry. Moving from friend to counselor isn't an easy task for a minister.

Entering Michael's study, I immediately noticed the chairs arranged around a table with a prominent box of tissue in the middle of it all. I reached for a handful and once more was lost in tears. I was too tired to care.

Ken began the conversation. I was quite struck by his openness and almost matter-of-fact way of saying what he had done. There was a part of me (hello, Fiddler) on the one hand that thought this wasn't easy for Ken, but, on the other hand, it looked easy for him. I was confused and angry.

Ken said, "I think the worst part of all this is over for me. I've decided the affair is over and I want to work on our marriage. The door is closed. But for you, Loyd, it's just beginning. I may be in denial, but that's what I think."

That was the first mention of "denial." The deeper we delved into how we got into this mess, the more denial on both of our parts was revealed.

Michael listened well to both of us. He was open with how shocked he was. We were the last people on earth he expected to see in his office with this type of problem! (I know; I was just as shocked to be sitting in his office.) He did say he had been aware the last time we were together he had felt an uneasiness. To him there had been some "red flags" signaling something was up.

Remembering what he was referring to, I felt embarrassed and humiliated. I said, "I feel so exposed and covered with muck!"

Pointing at me and punctuating each word with his finger, Michael said, "Don't wash it off. Dealing with the muck is one of your tasks."

We talked of how we were managing to be in the same house together. He suggested we might want to spend some time apart. He also said he believed Ken was dealing with "boy stuff." Old stuff that Ken hadn't been able to deal with completely was being raised up, not man-just-turned-60 stuff.

Michael challenged me with the importance of being clear about my limits— what I was willing to live with and what I would not tolerate. He leaned forward and looked at me and advised, "Keep him on the griddle. Keep it hot so he can get in there and work with it."

Turning to Ken he asked, "Do you think you can stand the heat?"

Without hesitation, Ken nodded his head, "Yes."

We agreed to return on Monday.

I felt the relief that comes from doing something. Michael had done a good job of listening to us and supporting both of us where we were. And we had done a good job as well. My fears were unfounded. I didn't have to listen to a laundry list of complaints, nor did Ken. We had taken a first step. Even though we were feeling very raw emotionally, we were as open as we knew how to be.

On the drive home, Ken and I talked about Michael's suggestion that we spend some time apart. Our friends were in agreement with Michael. Most believed, to be able to work things out, you needed to be apart. I could see their point of view. Some friends had said they couldn't understand how I could stand being in the same house with Ken, much less speak to him. I didn't bother to mention to anyone we were still sharing the same bed.

Perhaps our friends were right, but then they weren't us. Certainly if staying together wasn't working, we would find out pretty quickly. Ken was my best friend. I couldn't imagine not having him around to work all this out with. It was so odd one minute to want to talk with him, have him close to share my feelings, and hear from him as well, and then in the next minute realize this was the man who with cold calculation decided to have an affair. So confusing.

10.

The Third Day

I was beginning to wonder if there were something wrong with me. I thought it must be strange that it never occurred to me to ask Ken to leave. It didn't enter my mind. A few years ago I think I would have pitched him out and refused to talk to him except through my lawyer. Had I changed that much? Or was I in denial?

It had been three days. It felt like three years.

I roamed through the house into the wee hours of the morning caught up in blame. This time I was blaming myself, playing the "if only" game. I kept thinking I never should have shared my struggles with menopause with Ken. I shouldn't have told him my sexual feelings were close to zero sometimes. I wasn't passionate about making love—arousal was slow in coming. It was all my fault. I was not enough for him. He wanted more and I didn't know if I could give him what he wanted. It was all my fault. I drove him to her.

Finally falling asleep, I woke up at 5 a.m. feeling weak and lonely. I came back into the living room and wailed and cried. I am such a visual person. Pictures of Ken and Jane flashed into my head. Scenarios of their love-making hurt me to the point of nausea. For my sake, Ken thoughtfully never gave me any details of their meetings; the pictures were all being created in my own head. Annie said I could learn to cancel out the pictures. So "Cancel! Cancel! Cancel!" Would this ever go away, or was I forever going to be tortured by this?

There was only silence to answer my questions—just the steady ticking of the old clock; not even Taylor barked his complaints.

11.

Our Children's Compassion

Annie and Brian had decided to take a personal day off from work and spend a long weekend with us. Their visit could really be tough. They were both furious with Ken. I was not up for a weekend of battles. Sleep eluded me. Food was tasteless. I was not sure this was a good idea.

Talking to them on the phone the night before their visit, I told them I wasn't willing for them to come up if it was going to be three against one. Also I wanted them to know if it turned into open warfare, they were to go back home to Atlanta. To their credit they had already decided no battles. Brian said, "Mom, we just want to be there with the two of you."

Ken wasn't home when the children signaled their arrival by beeping their horn. With the dogs leaping around us, we hugged and made small talk as we unloaded their car. As always, Annie had her pile of dirty laundry with her—there's no place like home. Brian traveled light—a plastic bag with a change of clothes and a book. I need to take lessons from him.

Once settled in, the children and I talked. I was feeling apprehensive, afraid, and not wanting to deal with their upset or my own. I don't always get what I want.

In retrospect, I think I have spent a lot of time dealing with upsets in our family. Unlike my family of origin, the upsets in this household are for the most part loud and out in the open rather than underground and quiet. Of course, the irony in this present upset was that Ken chose to be underground and quiet. In my family I never heard "raised voices"—that's a Southern euphemism for arguing. When I was growing up, slammed doors, shouting, or anything that could be viewed as openly working out a conflict just didn't happen.

I can still hear my mother saying to me, "Change your tone of voice." I knew she not only wanted me to change my tone of voice, but she wanted me to keep the peace.

Silence was the unspoken rule in the house I grew up in. It was the type of silence filled with the energy of discontent, fueled by the knowledge that you had best join into the silence if you wanted peace to reign. There was a sense of being ill at ease that often ran underneath our life together. As a child I didn't understand why there was discomfort between my mother and father. Never was anyone in my family ever threatened with physical violence nor do I think there was a possibility of it erupting. Nonetheless, I felt the silence's effect as surely as if I had been hit in my solar plexus.

Dinnertime was the worst time. Gathered around the table, my mother, father, sister, and I ate in silence. The click of the forks on the plates was the only sound that could be heard. Grim. What conversation took place was inconsequential. No sharing of the day or world events, no relaxed patter, just silence. It is a wonder I didn't grow up with chronic indigestion!

I envied the liveliness I experienced at my friends' tables. I determined when I grew up and had a family of my own, the dinner table would be a center of sharing—a place of fun and openness allowing for the possibility we could at least listen to each other, cry, fight, laugh. Whatever was going on at the moment would be fair game for discussion. Ken and I have created just such a dinner table and, as I have mentioned, the kitchen table is also the site of much living in our home.

The children and I were sitting around the kitchen table when Ken came home. Coming up the stairs, he looked at me. He looked scared. I felt for him. I'm sure he must have believed he was walking into the lion's den.

I thought, "What a brave man. He could be eaten alive and he still came home."

The tension crackled about the room and our conversation was stilted. Everyone exchanged the usual pleasantries, "How are you?" "I'm fine." What a joke. There is nothing like being brought up a Southerner. We were going to be "nice" to each other even if it killed us.

It took a while for the natural warmth and love we have for each other to thaw out the tension. Questions were asked—questions that often didn't have answers or answers that Ken had figured out. What I noticed in our conversation that afternoon was Ken's willingness to answer anything they wanted to know. Gradually everything came out in the open.

Brian and Annie both noticed a difference in Ken's behavior.

Late in the afternoon Annie said, "Daddy, I don't ever remember you listening in the way you are listening to us now."

"How so?"

"You're present with us in a way we haven't ever experienced," Brian explained.

Easily distracted, Ken tends to be aware of everything around him as though he has invisible antennae growing out of his head. Often I would sense he was listening to me with only a fraction of himself while the rest of him was taking in whatever else was around. If the newspaper was within sight, he would be gazing at it while stroking Dickens and planning his next golf game. He would also be listening to anyone who was talking—often me. Several years ago Ken was diagnosed with attention deficit disorder (ADD); that made it hard for him to focus on one thing over a long period of time—and we talked a long time that afternoon.

12.

The Witch

After dinner Brian built a fire and suggested we play Hearts—play Hearts, what irony!

Brian knows I enjoy playing cards. It was thoughtful and a great idea. It would be a relief to sit around the card table. We laughed and teased—and went through the rules of the game. I almost felt normal.

Who would get the queen of spades, the unwanted witch? Would I go for it and shoot the moon? It would mean screwing up my courage, paying attention, and using the cards I'd been dealt—sounds like the game of life.

Several hands into the game, Annie suddenly burst into tears. "Mom, I have never heard you be so mean. You have done nothing but dig at Daddy all through dinner and now again playing cards. I can't stand it."

I was stunned. I hadn't realized how obvious I was. I had been aware of my anger, but, of course, I thought I was doing a great job of covering it up. So much for my acting ability.

She continued, "I feel so uncomfortable around you. I am not used to you being so negative. Why are you doing this?"

Filling up with tears, I replied, "Truthfully? I am miserable and I want your dad to be miserable too. I guess I want to punish him. I'm not used to this either. I don't want it this way, and I don't want you or anyone else feeling uncomfortable around me. I hate it. Keep calling me on the digs or anything else that smacks of how you know I don't want to be."

Turning to Ken, Annie asked, "Daddy, why are you not responding when Mom digs at you?"

Looking up from his cards, he replied, "She hasn't said anything that wasn't right on. Maybe I *want* to be punished. But it isn't getting to me like it is you, Annie."

Brian calmly played his hand and proceeded to shoot the moon while I, the witch, held onto the queen of spades.

13.

Role Reversal

I had a restless night. At one point I got up and went into the cabin. I was too tired to get out my journal and write. I think I just needed to soak up the comforting energy the cabin exudes. I looked through some magazines, stared into space, thought about the day's events, appreciated the sensitivity of our children, and went back to bed.

I woke up feeling scared and sick to my stomach. I couldn't seem to get beyond the early morning yuks. This time my mind was zeroing in on how Ken used my love and trust. I could never do that to him, so how could he do that to me? Does the deep sense of betrayal ever ease? It is all so unfathomable to me. He continues to be amazed at how hurt I am. And I continue to be amazed at how he could be so centered on himself.

It is as if a part of my being has been surgically removed without anesthesia.

Has my innocence been removed?

Or is it some sort of belief that this could never happen to me?

Was I naive to trust him or anyone else so implicitly?

Or am I just plain stupid and blind as a bat, not seeing how unlovable I actually am?

My chest ached as I went up the stairs to Annie's room. Her door was ajar. I peeked in to see if she was awake. She rolled over and looked up at me. All in one motion Annie pulled back the covers and opened up her arms to me. In that act our already close relationship went to a level we did not know was possible. It was a pivotal moment in which the daughter became the mother and the mother became the daughter.

I cried loud gut-wrenching tears of hurt and rage. Annie listened and held on. I poured out my anguish, despair, hurt, and the fear that Ken would never change. I hated being put through all this. I hated Ken's behavior. I hated the woman who participated. I hated it all. When I finally quieted down, Annie said, "Mom, have you ever thought how much this sounds like a soap opera?"

I reluctantly agreed with her.

"I also think," I said smugly, "I just got a partial payment for all the times I have listened and held you when you played out your own soap operas!"

Just like two teenagers at a slumber party, we broke into gales of laughter. Was this all too unreal or what?

David called sometime after breakfast. He was in a better place than in our last conversation.

It was easy talking to him and easy to use the opportunity to remind him how much I loved him. Our relationship had had its difficulties, and I was able to let him know I was sorry about that. Aware of my own wounds, it was important for me to go about healing any wounds that might still be between us.

He said, "Mom, I can't think of anything more wonderful than marrying a woman just like you."

14.

Coming Clean

The day was wrapped in the profound. It is difficult to describe. It was as if we had stepped into a power spot. I can't help but think, resting below us, the cave was working its magic, sending us all healing energy. Enveloped in this energy, our conversations around the fire and the kitchen table were like fine linen—to be treasured. There was also silence, comfortable and welcome.

One of our longer conversations was about "being in integrity" and what that meant to each of us. Visibly upset, Ken shared he was beginning to see how seduced he had been by the power of his own denial. Denial makes it easy to justify anything we want to do. Of course, I sat there self-righteously sure Ken's behavior was as far out of integrity as one could get. I was spotless, no break in my seamless picture of myself.

Eventually we dipped deeper into the subtleties of integrity. We talked about how easy it is to overlook so-called "small" things when you have lulled yourself into unawareness. For instance, taking paper clips or stamps from the office—no big deal. Really? The company can afford it, we justify—one of the perks of the job. Small action, but costly. I read somewhere that companies lose thousands of dollars each year from theft by their employees. Does it occur to any of us the real cost is to our heart of hearts—the human spirit?

Sitting around the fire that morning we enjoyed an easy flow of philosophical give and take. Each of us admitted there was no denying we knew when we were out of alignment with our integrity. It is no secret. It isn't as though we innocently don't have a clue. We know. Often it is manifested in not telling the truth. Where were the four of us not telling the truth to each other?

I thought, "Now we have stopped philosophizing and gone to meddling!"

The mood changed. Philosophizing was one thing, but putting the thoughts into action was another. Annie and Brian ended up doing some "clean-up work," confessing ways they had not been truthful with us. Nothing huge, but nonetheless, they clearly wanted no separation from us. I was touched and moved by their caring. What an example to set for Ken and me, for there was much "clean-up work" we needed to do if we were to stay in this relationship.

During my late morning shower, I had an "Aha!" Showers are a great source of revelation and creativity for me. I think some of my best thoughts when the water is pouring over me.

This morning was no exception. It occurred to me I had some confessing of my own to do. I wasn't so spotless after all. Funny how easy it is to forget completely what you don't want to remember.

Getting dressed I realized I had felt more anxious in the last five days than I had in my whole lifetime. I would go to bed feeling anxious. I would wake up feeling anxious. Off and on during the day I would feel anxious. I was sure the root of the anxiety was fear. Fear is a deadly thing. Twice I had thought of how I could kill myself and be rid of all the pain. Never before had it entered my mind to do away with myself as a solution to my feelings, but then, I hadn't been faced with such devastating feelings before.

With my stomach in now familiar knots, I headed into the living room for my own truth telling. Someone has said, "If you are scared, do it anyway." This would be tough.

15.

The Secret

Annie was curled up on the sofa reading with Clio, who was sleeping stretched out in a belly-up position by her side. Ken and Brian were equally engrossed in what they were reading. Dickens was nestled in one of his favorite spots, wedged between Ken and the chair. Such a great scene of domestic bliss. The sun shining in the cabin windows, warm and inviting, emphasized the relaxed tone of the sight.

"Ken, I realized during my shower I have something important I need to tell you," I said as I sat down in a nearby chair feeling very uncomfortable.

Annie looked up from her book and said, "Would you like for Brian and me to leave so you can talk?"

"No, there is no reason why you can't hear this too."

"What is it?" Ken asked, with curiosity in his voice.

Taking in a deep breath, I blurted out, "Tuesday morning I followed my hunch and read your journal."

Ken turned pale.

I could feel my stomach churn remembering how hard my heart was beating when I picked up the journal. He had left it out on his desk in plain sight. Maybe he had wanted me to read it. Even so, for me to read his private journal was breaking an extremely important commitment. We started using journals years ago as a means of expressing ourselves privately. I am big on "keeping my word," and I broke it big. I felt ashamed. Now he couldn't trust me either. So much for my seamless picture of myself.

I continued, "Reading your journal is how I knew for sure you were having an affair. I read it all—the poem you wrote her, meetings you had with her when I was around and when I was out of town. The phone calls when you said you were working downstairs. The lies you dreamed up to tell me. How you felt about making love to me. The driving back from Atlanta with her. I read it all."

Ken sat quietly soaking in my confession, "Anything more you want to say?"

"I feel ashamed, embarrassed. I wouldn't want you to read my journal, yet I read yours. I won't do it again and I apologize." I paused, "At the same time, I'm glad I know and I am not sure I would have if I hadn't read it. Will you forgive me?"

His response was immediate, "Of course, I forgive you. I don't like that you read it and I wish you hadn't read *all* of it, but once you started, I can see why you kept reading." He took off his glasses and rubbed his eyes for a moment. Putting his glasses back in place, he looked at me and said, "My fear is that you won't forgive *me* and you'll keep feeling hurt remembering all you read."

I felt dejected and could only manage to talk just above a whisper. I said, "I'm working on the forgiveness and I want the hurt to go away too, but I have no idea when that will be."

I was filled with anguish. "I do know I am tired—very tired and feeling anxious and sick to my stomach most of the time. I keep having images of you and Jane together and it just eats me up."

Annie spoke up, "Mom, you can handle that part easily. Remember I told you to simply say to yourself, 'Cancel, cancel, cancel'? Make yourself stop the visualization that is bothering you and replace it with a totally different image— like a map of Italy. I have used it over and over again when I have images of the truck that hit me years ago, and I use it whenever I hear car brakes screech. It works, believe me. If it is eating you up and you don't want your mind to go to those images, do it."

Brian and Annie were solid rocks from the time they arrived to the time they left. Each continued to listen and challenge when either Ken or I got into our stuff. I was sad to see them go Sunday, but okay with it. What a weekend, intense at times but a holy, holy time. We had given the gift of our real selves, our humanity, to each other. It was blessed and redeemed by the love we have for one another.

Am I not a fortunate woman?

This surely is a part of the reason Ken had the affair. This incredible experience never would have happened without it. How strange life can be.

16.

The Laundry List

Monday dawned cold and dreary. I managed to stay in bed all night; that's a small miracle. Although I didn't sleep all the time, I didn't feel the need to get up and write.

Fear and anxiety raised their heads as soon as I opened my eyes. Ken expressed feeling it too, with an added dose of depression. Annie called this morning and is feeling depressed as well. I wonder if feelings float in the air like a virus? I wish whoever said, "This too shall pass" had added the words, "and quickly."

Today we have another appointment with Michael. I am glad we have him to go to, but I am looking forward to our therapist's return.

The afternoon appointment with Michael was an uncomfortable and revealing time for both Ken and me.

Michael had uncovered and latched onto a core belief of mine. Actually, there were two that came to light; perhaps they are stepsisters. Neither was new to me, I just hadn't hooked them up with how I had been feeling. Nothing like surprises that creep through the back door and bite you.

The first belief was that I am "not enough"—specifically, I am not enough sexually for Ken. His roaming eye throughout our marriage and other indications that emphasized my lack in that department made it easy for my conclusion. The affair put the nail in the coffin. I had no doubt now I was "not enough."

Coupled with "not enough" was the belief that I was not wanted. Getting in touch with that oldie was a shock.

Michael was pushing on my "not enough" when he asked, "How far back does this belief go?"

"Oh, I can trace it back to early in our marriage."

"Where else have you felt 'not enough'?"

I pondered a bit, "No boyfriends come to mind. Daddy thought I was wonderful."

Michael nodded, "And how about your mother?"

Kaboom!

Tears flowed, making good use of the tissue on the table again.

"I honestly believe she didn't want me. My sister Ann was seven years old when I was born. From stories around Ann's birth, I think Mother suffered from postpartum blues, something they knew very little about in those days. I don't think she wanted another child after Ann."

I blew my nose and continued, "As an adult, I went so far as to ask Mother and Daddy about the seven years difference between Ann and me. All I got were blank looks. Also, with a name like Loyd, every time anyone met me I would hear, 'So your parents wanted a boy.' I felt like one big disappointment all the way around."

Michael asked, "Do you think they wanted a boy?"

"No, not really. Loyd was my mother's maiden name. I was a teenager before I met a boy named Lloyd; of course it was usually spelled with two l's. I finally understood why people who met me assumed it was a boy's name. I just thought they were stupid and didn't get it when I had explained it. In reality, though, I think those encounters were the seed bed of my thinking maybe they *did* want a boy. I could easily have taken it to heart."

It was clear I had work to do. Getting down under all those feelings and focusing on what is really true is hard labor. I also think it isn't wise to labor alone. With that in mind, I planned to meet with a friend. As if I didn't have enough of a laundry list of work to do, these were two more tasks needing to be handled.

Ken had his own laundry list. His cover of denial was very obvious to him. He couldn't believe how he had justified his behavior. It was as though someone else had acted instead of Ken. Some of his fears were around the "scandal" he believed he had created. Though there was no actual scandal, Michael suggested that Ken, even though he was a retired priest, talk with the bishop about his thoughts and fears, which Ken did. The bishop was grateful to be included in our life, prayed for us, and sent us on our way.

When we arrived home, we checked our voice mail. My stomach flipped over when I heard a familiar caring voice. One of our mentors, Brad Brown, a friend who had taught us so much in the many courses we had taken from him, had returned our call.

Both of us were excited. If ever there was someone we knew would support us and give us guidance from his heart, it was Brad.

17.

Different Levels

Reaching Brad at his home, we brought him up to date. We voiced our concern about whether staying together here at home was the right decision and wondered whether we were being blinded by our desire to be together. Since he knew us well, we asked for his take on it.

Brad didn't hesitate.

"Choose for yourselves what you want, not what other people want," he advised. "It is easy for even your most helpful friends to operate out of their own stuff—their own thoughts of what *they* would do if they were faced with the same decision. Separating is the *'world's'* way of dealing with an affair. You forget you are working on a different level."

Lovingly, he praised Ken on his lack of ambivalence. "Ambivalence could cause Loyd to flounder around and come to decisions of what she needs on her own. You have major work ahead, but, Ken, I think you will be a happy man for having hung in there."

Finally Brad added, "Loyd, you are fine. Remember the exercise I taught you that brings you home to yourself? Practice taking a deep breath, go up on your toes, then go down on your heels, and see if that doesn't help you settle and more easily come from that place of home—the deepest part of you. It looks as though Ken was threatened in some way by you. You might want to look at how you have made that easy for him."

Sigh, one more item to go on my laundry list.

However, I felt a lifting of my spirits hearing Brad's thoughts. It had not occurred to me that we were "working at a different level," as Brad put it. I understood what he meant. We had done much inner work through the years. I was not willing to sit in the place or at the level of where we had been. I was going to say that level looked dark, but that isn't right. It was gray. I realized I had been sitting in a gray place for a long time, moving through my life unaware of the colors and light in our relationship.

Where had all the color and light gone?

PART II: THE CHRYSALIS

18.

Morning Despair

February is over today—not the best of months and a hell of a year so far. Stayed in bed and slept most of the night. It is amazing that that would be so important, but it is.

Last night before bed, I felt such despair. It had dawned on me what a heady feeling for Ken—two women in love with him and wanting him.

I asked him how it is to have two women wanting him. He laughed and said, "A boost for the old ego!" I thought to myself, "What a cost to boost your ego."

I woke up wanting Ken to take me in his arms, tell me it's all right, how much he loves me, how beautiful I am, tenderly touch me and be with me. Of course, he had no clue that's what I wanted and I couldn't tell him. Why is that? Am I afraid he will think I am so needy he will be totally turned off? I need to practice asking for what I want.

Ken plods ahead doing various tasks, eating, walking the dogs. I know he too is depressed. I asked him how he gets himself to move. All I want to do is lie in bed with the covers over my head.

Lying down on the bed with me, he talked about his depression. It took him years to realize he had believed that to be Ken meant to be depressed. It took him more years to discover that the type of depression he has, recurring depression, is organic and can be helped with medication as well as therapy. The therapist he went to for years spoke of depression as having a kindling effect. It kindled itself and kept itself burning. Ken said he had learned that movement—doing something—had an un-kindling effect even if it was just getting up and brushing his teeth.

We talked more about what I had said last night about being loved by two women. He can move in any direction, and he will still be worshipped and adored.

Really ticks me off! I can't do that. I don't feel worshipped and adored by anyone. I don't know if I ever have. What feels worse is I am not even sure he has the capacity to do that with me—just with her. Why would he even want to stay with me when he has someone foaming at the mouth to be with him? I certainly am not foaming at the mouth to be with him.

This is not a good morning! I don't even feel like moving to brush my teeth or anything else!

19.

Pulling Out All the Stops—Not Allowed

Ken decided to take the weekend off to play golf with our sons. Brian drove up from Atlanta with David, who flew in from Colorado to join them. They headed for warmer climates—both literally and figuratively. Ken needed the warmer climate, and we both needed the distance of some miles between us.

I felt relieved to have some time alone. I also felt a little scared. It had been tough for the both of us, the last few days in particular.

Why is it when either of us goes out of town, we often fight or get irritated with each other before one or the other leaves? This parting was no exception.

It went something like this:

Ken was out walking the dogs and I was taking a shower. As I stood in the shower, tears began to wash me as well. Showers are a great place to cry. Unfortunately Ken walked into the bathroom and heard me sobbing away.

He stormed out of the room shouting, "You are like a wounded animal. I will be so glad when you get over this."

While I was dressing, he returned with a foam rubber bat in his hand. "Here! Beat me; hit me. Beat me up with this." Waving the bat in big motions, "You need to stop all this."

If we hadn't been so deadly serious, the whole scene would have been hilarious—Ken prancing around the room swinging a bat with me half-dressed watching him. But I was not amused and unable to take the bat.

Throwing it across the room, he shouted, "And I don't want you to be alone in this house while I am gone."

Facing him, I shouted back, "I want to be alone. I want to be able to cry, scream, rant and rave without you telling me to get over it. It's too bad if you don't want me to be alone!"

His shoulders sagged as he sat down on our bed. Through his own tears he said, "I know you aren't beating me up. It is just so hard seeing you hurting. I keep telling myself it is an important process for you to go through and we don't know how long it will take. It's just that I am so tired of all of this and I feel so bad about it all."

Sitting down on the bed beside him, I said, "Ken, I have spent a lot of years hiding my feelings. Not only from you, but from me. I think you've done the same thing. I believe it is one of the things we need to change. It hasn't been okay for me or you to pull out all the stops."

He admitted, "I think you're right. It always seems to scare you when I get angry or even when I get really excited about something."

We had spent more time talking in the last week than we had in years. The change had been good but also frustrating. Ken saw us not getting anywhere and I didn't think there was anywhere to get, yet. Both of us were looking forward to John's return from Costa Rica.

Were we looking for a "fix"?

Probably so. I was thinking a "fix" would be divine. John certainly had his work cut out for him.

20.

On My Own

My mind goes nuts thinking I will drive Ken away with my pain. Somehow I have to not let him see it—stuff it—work on it when he isn't around.

God, how could You? How could You allow such a terrible thing to happen to me? I have done nothing to deserve such betrayal. You should have prevented it! You should make Ken and Jane suffer for their behavior, their cruelty, their lies, and they should know it came directly from You! Why didn't You stop it? What kind of God are You? Where were You when I needed You?

In the process of writing out my hurt, anger, frustrations, revengeful thinking, I can actually feel some lightness. My heart doesn't ache so much— literally and figuratively. I see some of the stuff that is wrapped around my heart making it hard and closed. I do not want to live my life this way. I am not a closed, hard-hearted, revengeful person. I know the way out is forgiveness, but I can't seem to get there.

Annie shared with me on the phone last night her lack of anger at her daddy. Instead she is furious with me. She can't understand why I have hung in there with her dad for so long. "It's your life," she pointed out.

She sees her father as someone who has often taken advantage of me in the past. She brought up old reminders of times she had confronted him with what she saw. For her, the affair was the ultimate, and the fact that I didn't move on and take care of myself angered her.

She is right. He has taken advantage of me from time to time and, truthfully, I of him. Sometimes I simply have been blind to it. Is that part of being in a relationship—you become blind? So much has to do with the intent, the attitude behind it all. As far as the affair is concerned, the intent was to deceive me and take full advantage of my love and trust. Pretty blatant stuff. All of this is fuel for resentment to flourish.

What she doesn't see is the Ken I live with on a day-to-day basis. My experience of Ken's sweetness, his warmth and caring is covered up by her father-daughter stuff. I trust she will work all that out in time. The circumstances we are living in at the moment don't make it easy for any of us, Ken included.

Seeing the taillights of Ken's car go down the driveway, I had a momentary jolt of fear. "This is the first time we have been apart," I thought. Breathing in, I realized it wasn't fear I was feeling but excitement—a lost feeling regained.

I had the whole weekend to take care of just me. No one to feed, no one to mesh my schedule with, and no one to talk to or argue with, except the dogs. Responding to my thought, Dickens popped through the doggie door into the living room. He had been hanging over the edge of the deck watching Ken go down the driveway too. From the bounce of his step he seemed pleased as well. The house would be free of tension for awhile.

The afternoon went quickly and I settled down for the evening. With nothing more than a snack for supper, I decided to take a bubble bath and soak my soul, maybe even turn on the Jacuzzi.™

I love our bathroom. It is a great space for unwinding. The shower is large and roomy with two shower heads so we can shower together. An antique pine buffet worn by years of service has a hole cut in the center for the bathroom sink. With the legs removed and its deep drawers, no one would ever know it wasn't designed for its new purpose. Above the sink hangs a large mirror with rhododendron limbs gracefully framing it. In amongst the limbs I have wrapped tiny Christmas lights making the whole mirror look magical. The wooden floor reflects the tiny lights and glowing candles, creating a warm atmosphere.

Tucked in the corner near the tub is a cozy chair. It is a great place to look out over the valley as you take off your clothes or floss your teeth or just stare out into the world. At the moment the chair was full of the dogs anticipating my stay in the tub. Dickens loved to lie by the side of the tub in the hope the Jacuzzi™ would be turned on. Then to his delight, he would listen to the hum of the motor and catch a lick of the bubbles—such a boy dog. Clio, however, preferred to lie curled up in the chair. If I turned on the Jacuzzi™ she would run and hide under the bed, no motor noises for her.

Armed with a glass of wine, I lit the candles in the bathroom and breathed in the scent of lavender floating up from the tub. Easing my way into the warm water I noticed the city lights below and rejoiced in the view through the bare trees. Much to my amazement I felt happy. Could this be a new trend?

With bubbles up to my chin, I began to feel my body relax. "I should do this every night—a gift to me from me," I said, smiling to myself.

21.

Empty-Handed

The next morning I decided to venture into town and look for a book. I often rely on books for support. Sometimes I can read my way into action or a new way of thinking. I worked in a bookstore years ago, and just walking into one and inhaling the unmistakable odor of books pleasures me. However, pleasure seemed to avoid me this time.

I was looking for a book about "How to Deal with an Affair" or anything that came close to that title. In our local bookstore, I saw nothing remotely resembling anything I thought would be helpful. I was expecting it to fall into my hands as so often happened in the past. No such luck.

When I got back to my car, I realized I was feeling incredibly uncomfortable. I felt nervous—my heart was beating fast and my palms felt sweaty. There was something about looking in the self-help section that announced to everyone in the store what a failure I was. It was even louder than that. Standing in the self-help aisle was some sort of trumpet blast to the world! It was as though I had a sign on me that read, "This pitiful woman's husband had an affair, and you can just look at her and see why!"

With zero results from the first store, I screwed up my courage and drove into Asheville. I was determined not to let my feelings towards Jane stop me from living my life, but it was hard! I was so afraid of running into her. What if I picked the very bookstore, the very day Jane decided to look for a book with the same title? Believe me, I didn't see the humor in that question that I do now. I really thought it was possible! Fear does incredible things to your mind—and who knows, it could have happened.

With anxiety galore I drove to two large bookstores. No book. I was convinced the search was hopeless. Unable to ask a salesperson for help, I came home empty-handed. I believe the books were there, but I wasn't in the place to see them.

Once home, I took the dogs for a long walk to clear my upset. It was cold and windy. The dogs were eager to forge ahead with noses to the ground checking on all the various scents. I thought about spring coming and the comfort of the cycle of nature. The ferns will reappear, their fronds unfolding as regular as clockwork. I shall return as well. Clio turned to look at me with her ears back in loving recognition. To her I have never left.

Our mountain is blessed with an abundance of wildflowers and creatures. We are on the migratory path of the Monarch butterfly and, though Ken and I haven't had the experience, one of our neighbors described to us seeing her trees and shrubs drip with butterflies. What a sight that must have been. Birds flock to our feeders all year round. A pair of pileated woodpeckers astound us every time they appear announcing their arrival with weird giggles. Great horned owls, screech owls, a wonderful growing family of ruffed grouse, an occasional fox, as well as the usual raccoons, opossums, and squirrels roam about day and night. One evening we were returning from somewhere when funny wild turkeys with their ostrich-like walk stopped us cold on the road. All manner of unseen animals roam the old logging paths. I have been told there was a time when panthers walked these mountains. Bears have been sighted as well. As Dorothy and her cohorts in Oz said, "Lions and tigers and bears, oh my."

The road was clear of creatures and so was my mind. The dogs scampered up the last hill for home, and I was grateful for remembering the love I have of this land and all who travel it.

22.

The Angry Phone Call

For some, curling up in a favorite chair listening to classical music, perhaps lighting the fire, and sipping a comforting tea are totally healing—expecting nothing, doing nothing, just being. For me, curling up in *my* favorite chair, all the above, the music, the tea, the fire *and* writing in my journal are frequently roads to healing for me. I am not a constant journal writer, but when I am troubled or need to work something out, I find my chair is the perfect spot.

My chair sits in our bedroom next to the fireplace. It is one of those chairs made for two, not as big as a loveseat but roomy with a large cushion that supports my back just so. The back cushion is also a favorite hangout for the dogs—so much so that it has a permanent dent where some lazy dog snoozed away part of his day.

With my weekend fast approaching its end, my chair called to me. It was time to do some writing—putting on paper those things that roll around in my mind and get to me—things I say "cancel, cancel, cancel" to, which don't ever seem to want to be canceled.

I have learned through workshops I have taken, books I've read, and enlightened friends that writing down and letting go of painful garbage is imperative to having a healthy body and a healthy mind. Deepak Chopra, among many others, says, "The secret to perfect health is choosing it." I chose health in mind, body, and spirit. I refused to let my pain destroy me.

I wrote until the early morning hours. In particular, I wrote down grievances, resentments—things I thought were unfair and cruel. I had already filled pages n my journal in the days before, but tonight I was on a roll. Often out of my pen would come raw meat; venomous, hate-filled words; revengeful thinking. Not the sort of thing I want anyone to read. Some of my thoughts shocked me. I had never tapped into the depth of this stream of ugliness. However, it was the truth. Sadly, it was how I was thinking.

Anger dripped from every word. I wrote nasty notes to Jane and to everyone else I thought might have had a part in enabling all that happened. I had quite a 'hate" list—and God was at the head of the it!

I finally put my pen down at 2 a.m. Blessed sleep arrived at last. Dickens woke me up at five barking in his sleep, funny muffled sounds accompanied by twitching legs. I fell back to sleep and woke up with the radio playing. It had been playing for fifteen minutes before I heard it. Good for me.

Outside it looked like a winter wonderland. There was ice on the trees and a heavy glaze on the deck. The ice would be short-lived. The icicles rimming the roof of the cabin were already melting in the warmth of the sun. The poor rhododendron leaves had rolled tightly into pencil shapes to protest the cold. A bird was singing, oblivious to the cold. The dogs and I were still curled up in the bed—how luxurious. It was 7:54 and I longed to hear from Ken.

Up at last, the dogs and I had been fed and watered. To complete the morning's routine, Dickens rounded me up to make the trip down to the mailbox to get the paper. He and I took such comfort in the patterns of the morning. The ice had melted enough for me to attempt the drive, so off we went. Only a few trees were bent over the road heavy with their coat of ice, but they were easy to drive around and our mission was successful, although we saw no rabbits or squirrels along the way to entertain Dickens and to make it a totally worthwhile journey for him.

With my cup of tea I settled in the cabin to lose myself in the Sunday paper. Everyone was in his place, Clio snuggling up to my side and Dickens soaking up the morning sun on the back of the sofa.

BEYOND THE AFFAIR

The phone rang. It was Ken. Earlier I had longed to hear his voice, but hearing it now, I felt myself bristle. What was my problem?

We had talked Saturday morning, and neither of us had enjoyed the conversation. We had picked at each other and had ended the call just short of slamming the phone down, blaming one another for nothing in particular. He was upset, I was upset, and, of course, his golf game was awful. He thought it was all my fault, and I thought it was all his fault. I think it would have been smart to have agreed to a moratorium and not talked until he came home. Hindsight is wonderful.

This conversation wasn't much better. His anger was close to the surface as he talked about how poorly he had played. I could have decided to hang up, but I didn't. He didn't ask how I was. Was I having a good day? And, in my resentment, I didn't volunteer. Neither did I sympathize with him about his golf. So goes war—neither side willing to talk about what is actually going on. Pretty grim.

I hung up marveling over our anger seething underneath the few things we said to each other. Our lack of tenderness to one another was appalling. The question of whether we were going to make it loomed large, filling up the whole cabin.

At times I thought I was walking in slow motion through the rooms of the cabin and my life. I was caught inside some strange opaque balloon, pushing the balloon walls out as I went. During those times I was intent on looking straight ahead. I saw no colors—nothing. I also got the sense that I was walking in place. It was trudge, trudge, trudge—hard work, endless, exhausting—getting nowhere.

I was depressed.

I awoke from my brooding with a determination not to get sucked into the pits of despair. It looked as if I was trying to sabotage the end of my weekend. Besides, I reminded myself, in reality I had nothing to despair about. When was

I going to accept that any way this marriage went I was okay? "Perhaps when the pain in my chest goes away," I thought, absentmindedly rubbing my chest.

Ken had said movement helped break the kindling effect of depression, so I put the paper down, put on some music, and moved! I spent the rest of the morning sprucing up the cabin, singing at the top of my lungs "Young At Heart" with Jimmy Durante and his gravelly voice. Sure enough, just as Ken said, my depression lifted and soothed my gravelly mind.

23.

Feathers and Light

Happy, and with a neat cabin, I put on my jacket and headed outside. The winter air was crisp with no wind to blow through me. The ice had all melted. However, my trusted thermometer, the end of my nose, was cold, telling me it was much colder than I had thought it was. Clio and Dickens ran before me with only an occasional backward look. The leaves made a thick carpet in the woods, warming all the plants beneath them. Bare trees were strikingly beautiful standing in their stark, graceful lines. Views of the mountain ranges, round and soft, treated me throughout our walk.

Whenever I walk, I always keep an eye peeled for the unusual. Today it was a feather resting on the dirt road. I hadn't seen it on the walk down the mountain, but it was very apparent on the way up. Picking it up and rolling it over, I thought it looked like a pheasant's feather. I have never seen a live pheasant, only photographs. This feather would be perfect in the band of a hat a la 1940.

Smoothing the feather with my fingers as I walked, an idea began to form in my mind. I decided to create a little altar, a shrine to celebrate me. A place to soothe as well as spark me. Every time I walked by it, I wanted to see symbols of things that matter to me.

So where would I make this altar?

I arrived back at the house anticipating the hunt for this special place.

The cabin itself is a small snug space with low-beamed ceilings and beautiful round golden logs for walls. An altar would be pretty public there, and I didn't think I wanted that. I wandered around in thought, through the kitchen, maybe in the bathroom? No, I didn't want my altar there either.

I kept being pulled to our bedroom where my chair resides. Our bedroom is part of an addition we added after we had lived in the cabin six years or so. It has high ceilings, much more open than the cabin. Windows everywhere let in the view from all directions as well as lots of sun. The painter who painted all the window frames complained to our builder, "These folks have more windows in this addition than in that whole house you're building!" We obviously love the light and we have plenty of it.

I sat down in my chair and looked around the room. Where, oh where, would it be? I didn't want it to take up a lot of space or be something that bothered Ken. This was his room too. My eyes lit on the long pine table across from the foot of our bed and directly in front of four windows. Perfect.

The windows looked southeast. In the early morning the light would shine at an angle on my little altar. As I got up and stood at the table, the afternoon sun was casting long shadows of the nearby trees. I could imagine leaves shimmering and dancing in the center of the table creating an even more magical spot. This was definitely the place.

I spent the rest of the day playing with my altar.

I searched among my baskets and found a rarely used simple rattan tray. It became the sacred receptacle, the vessel, the keeper. Filling it almost full of all sizes of creamy champagne-colored candles, I stepped back to look at it. It looked so pretty I thought I might just stop there.

Tentatively, in the midst of the candles, I placed the pheasant feather and another small fluffy feather I had saved from an earlier walk. Their new nest fit them. I added a blue marble with a replica of the world on it, a small patchwork heart—very worn and loved, a carved wooden black angel, a crystal given to me

75

by a dear friend, and a tiny painted metal bird my mother gave me. Each sat like little jewels among the candles quite at home—me too. Much later I would add a small wooden oval Shaker box, which contained our beloved Dickens's ashes.

24.

Homecoming

It's Monday. Ken called. He's heading home and—whoopee!—he had a good golf game. I took responsibility for the anger I dumped on him yesterday and was relieved to share it with him and let it go.

I busied myself making soup and bread so I wouldn't have to deal with dinner later. I built a fire and enjoyed being in the living room all afternoon in front of it. I had nothing to do all day but read, let the dogs in and out, and soak in the quiet.

Around five I heard the car coming up the driveway. The dogs leapt from the sofa, tore through the kitchen, bounded down the stairs to the garage door. Their welcome was accentuated by barking and leaping, dancing and prancing, waiting for Ken to open the door. There is nothing like the greeting of delighted dogs. Though outwardly I wasn't dancing and leaping, inwardly my heart was keeping time with their antics as I looked forward to Ken stepping through the door.

I was so glad to see him. He looked refreshed, his face warm and soft. We kissed and I was fully with him and he with me. A lovely homecoming gift to us both.

We ate our dinner in front of the fire—talked and laughed.

I got to hear various tales about the golf games, how Brian and David are, and the fun they all had together. At the center of their fun was the infamous talcum powder golf ball that blows up when you hit it with your club. They have played this trick on one another before but always are surprised when it happens. David was set up to be the victim this go-around and ended up hitting not one but two talcum balls. Hitting one was funny enough, but two added to the hilarity.

This was the first time the men in the family have gone off together and played. It sounded like the trip was a great success and needs to be repeated at least once a year. How grand for them. Annie and I have enjoyed a number of "run away from home" trips. Now "the boys" can go play too.

Tomorrow we go to see John Hoover—our therapist is finally home from Costa Rica. Whenever I think about seeing him, I feel anxious, scared, and super-vulnerable yet I want to go. I am ready. I want to get to the bottom of what has happened—handle what I need to handle, and proceed forward for myself and our marriage. Of course, I want Ken to be ready and to want to move forward, but that is up to him. Always hanging out there is the question, will we make it through together or decide to go our separate ways?

Our trip to Knoxville through the foothills of the Smokies was quiet. I usually enjoy the beauty of these majestic mountains, but on this day it was totally lost on me. I was focused inward and feeling scared.

The "unknown" shifts its shape into monstrous sizes and implications when I am caught up in worry. My chest ached; my head ached. I had conversation after conversation with John in my head. Over and over, again and again, telling the story. Saying it this way, now that way, getting it "right," getting it "wrong." Although I knew intellectually the words didn't really matter, my gut believed what I had to say determined whether I would live or die.

Feeling raw and vulnerable, I arrived at John's office doorstep. I must have looked bedraggled— terror stricken and desperate, wanting to find the nearest window to escape through and fly away! I thought to myself, "Surely it will get better with each trip." But inwardly I knew better.

I cried through most of the two hours.

78

Ken began.

"John, when Loyd came to see you a few months ago, she thought she was going crazy. She was having difficulty dealing with my anger." Taking a deep breath, he continued, "You thought she was receiving mixed messages from me and you explained to her that mixed messages can make you feel crazy. You also asked her if she knew why this was happening. And she didn't." Looking over at me and back at John, he continued, "Well, what was happening was I was having an affair."

We were silent for a moment or two. Ken's words seemed to be sitting in the middle of the floor with us looking at them as though they were going to materialize.

John looked at the two of us and broke the silence. "What is your purpose in being here? What are you wanting?"

Talking through the huge lump in my throat, I said, "My purpose? What I want is to work on our marriage and come to a mutual decision whether we stay in our marriage or not. I need to know my part in all of this, and I need to look at how I make it easy for him to feel threatened because when that happens, Ken doesn't tell me the truth or he withholds what he is thinking."

Staring out into the room and feeling furious, I said, "I absolutely hate all of this!" I sobbed, "I still can't even believe this is happening. I know I am not willing to have a marriage if it isn't built on trust. I don't know how to regain that trust, and I don't know how we can mutually decide on whether we stay together or separate. I feel totally lost."

Another long pause.

"Ken, what is your purpose in coming here?" John repeated.

"Much the same as Loyd's, to work on our marriage and to decide what we're going to do. Plus I want to work through my sexual fears." With frustration in his voice, he continued, "For years I've worked in therapy and in other ways on my sexual fears and fantasies. And somehow I have never managed to make peace with them, conquer them, let go of them, or not have them be a burden to me."

With our purposes out on the table, John addressed my concern of how to decide mutually whether we stayed together or not.

"That's easy," he said. "We'll put the decision in a time frame of your choosing. Choose a date when you'll decide. Do you want to decide what direction you're going to take three months from now, six months, a year?"

"Well, I sure don't want it to take as long as a year," I offered.

Ken agreed and added his thoughts, "How about six months?"

"That sounds better to me," I agreed.

Throwing his hands up in the air, Ken said, "But what if I say something really upsetting to Loyd and she says, 'That's it!' and walks out? So much for setting a date."

"No, that's not how it will work," John replied. "I'll be the keeper of the date. Either of you can get as upset as you want. You can say anything you want. You can even walk out. But, nothing, *nothing*, will be decided until six months is up. Understand?"

We nodded our heads in agreement like two little children.

"So what's the date?" John asked with a broad smile on his face.

We looked at each other and reckoned six months would be September 7.

September 7 seemed light years away, but I was amazed at the wave of relief I felt. A ten-pound boulder had been lifted from my shoulders. John had taken on a part of my mind so occupied with trying to figure it all out that it was wearing *me* out. I no longer had to hold the "how" of it. John would do that.

My headache was gone.

25.

Ready to Ride

The world is fortunate to have a John Hoover in it. He is a man of great integrity and compassion. It is a great gift to enable his clients—me, in particular—to feel safe, accepted, loved, and challenged—and to see him makes me smile.

John is a big man, probably 6'3" or 6'4", bearded, warm, quick to hug you when he sees you, and with a mind like a steel trap. You can sense his centeredness, which is settling to be around. Though he is quiet and thoughtful, he isn't a quiet, stroke-his-beard type of therapist who says, "How does that make you feel?" John is more likely to jump out of his seat, take a magic marker, and begin to draw diagrams on newsprint in an effort to teach you visually how to recognize what is happening. Or he may scribble a communication exercise with arrows flying all over the page for you to see there is another way of doing something. (I still have several of his sheets of newsprint for reference.) I love his exuberance.

There is no doubt you are doing serious work with him, yet he is generous with his laughter. He also has a booming voice when he chooses to raise it to accentuate a point or to draw you out to express your feelings.

He starts with the now—what's happening now—and from there on out you are on a ride to the hills. I am forever grateful for his full participation with me and with Ken. It was unmistakably clear he was on the ride with us.

Ken and I made a commitment to John and to each other to travel the two and a half hours each way to therapy, two times a week, for us to resolve our differences. By September we would, hopefully, come to a decision as to what direction our lives would take.

This commitment, combined with our willingness to have our relationship as our first priority, and our determination to go full tilt with John's guidance, hurled us forward.

John said, "With your willingness to roll up your sleeves and go to work, you two are a therapist's dream come true."

Yes, we were ready to ride.

26.

A Log Cabin in Maine

The next item John undertook was Ken's sexual fears.

John believes that sexual feelings are always with a person —sometimes on full alert and other times not. Your sexual feelings are not *who* you are so much as a part of you, like a "companion" you carry around with you. "Does it make sense, Ken, to refer to your sexual feelings as your companion?"

"Yes, I think I am understanding you."

"So how is it for you to view women through the eyes of your companion?" John inquired.

Thinking about it for a moment, Ken answered, "Honestly, I get a certain amount of pleasure looking at women through my companion. I enjoy it. If I am not sexually attracted to a woman, I don't get into much of any kind of relationship with her."

"What about women you aren't sexually attracted to?" John pressed.

"Well, I don't like to admit it, but I don't particularly want to be around them."

John said, "I can see how looking at women only through your companion is a real burden to you. You never give yourself the opportunity to know the whole woman. Holding only to that view, the sexual turn-on is bondage."

John rose from the sofa and went to his newsprint easel and drew a small square in the upper right-hand corner of the paper.

Pointing to the square, he said, "This is a little log cabin in Maine." Next he drew an X at the center of the bottom of the paper, "This is you and your companion."

Settling back down on the sofa, John leaned forward and said, "Ken, I want you to practice containing your companion and sending it to that log cabin in Maine." Pointing again to the square, "To Maine."

"You can learn to contain your companion and to put it aside. I am *not* saying to ignore it, but contain it. Ship it off to Maine. Begin practicing this and see what viewing a whole woman is like. For instance, when you're in the drugstore, wherever, and you realize you are viewing a woman through your companion, stop yourself."

Sitting back, he said, "Ken, it may help you to understand you aren't the only man who views women only through his companion. Unfortunately, we men treat viewing women sexually as a form of permissible recreation we are entitled to play. By the way," looking over at me, "women do this too, but it is more often men than women."

He paused and looked back at Ken. "Do you think you can begin practicing this approach to dealing with your sexual feelings?"

"Oh, yes, it sounds helpful. Believe me, I'm ready to try anything. I don't want to constantly view women in this way. I give myself such a hard time for doing it and the bottom line is it's like treating women like 'objects'—no real appreciation of who they really are. And I think I miss a lot."

John turned to me and asked, "How are you doing with all of this?"

"It sure makes sense to me. What has struck me, as I have been listening, is why I have felt sexually unseen by Ken. He doesn't view me through his companion."

"What do you mean? I do too think of you sexually," Ken shot back.

"Okay, you think of me sexually. But my experience of you being with me is you see me sexually maybe one percent of the time. I would give anything if you looked at me the way you look at other women. I don't mean like an object, but with a twinkle in your eye. Well, more than a twinkle—with desire— with sexual energy behind it. Like you 'want me.'"

John, "So it's important to you for Ken to look at you sexually—send out sexual energy, to want you?"

"Sure." Turning to face Ken, I added, "Right now I don't see how I have any chance of having a sexual relationship with you, Ken. All this juicy stuff going on between you and Jane, secrecy and intrigue. As you have said, part of the excitement was sneaking around. You have none of that with me."

Rolling his eyes, Ken shook his head, "I can't win. I never can win."

27.

Indulging

We took a break and stretched our legs. There was tea in the waiting room, and I eagerly escaped John's office to refill my cup.

Back in our seats again, John said, "Ken, I want to get back to your never winning. What do you mean, you can never win?"

"I can see Loyd's point of view. Of course, our relationship isn't new nor does it have the kind of excitement that the affair had—that's why I say I can't win."

"Saying you can't win sounds like there is some sort of competition involved here," John surmised.

"No, I don't think I am talking about competition. For instance, when I am telling a story and Loyd interrupts me, it really hacks me off. I think she believes I can't tell the story right and has to correct me. When she does that, I think others believe I can't tell the story either."

"Loyd, when Ken is telling a story, do you interrupt because he can't tell the story?"

"I have interrupted him when I don't think he is telling the story right, but mostly I get involved with what he is saying. I am participating, adding in," I said.

"So you get a buzz out of the story and want to participate." Shifting back to Ken, he asked, "Are you wanting to win and Loyd lose?"

"Well, sure," he answered.

John said, "Sounds like competition to me. You see what she is doing through glasses of competition. You've got to win, or else others will think you don't know how to tell a good story."

Ken laughed, "I think you're right. I do see it as competition; no doubt I want to win."

"If you were to remove the glasses, you see a whole other thing. It's a lot like containing your companion—contained, you see something else. Both are 'indulgences.' Like your companion, competition is an 'add-on'—something extra you have added to the situation which isn't necessary except to give you pleasure—in this case at Loyd's expense."

John turned to me and explained, "You know there is a connection for you here when I talk about 'indulging.' One of the things you said earlier was that you thought you had been 'made a fool of.' You said all of what had happened had been going on behind your back and Ken and Jane had 'made a fool of you.'"

"Loyd, we didn't make a fool of you. You aren't a fool. We didn't set out to 'make a fool of you,'" Ken interrupted.

Continuing, John said to me, "It is important work for you to separate out what *is* true about you. Your trust *has* been broken. You *do* feel betrayed, injured, and raw. That is the truth. Being 'made a fool of' is an add-on, an 'indulgence,' causing you to suffer unnecessarily. In other words, there is enough true pain for you to deal with without your indulging in the untrue belief you have been 'made a fool of.'"

I could hear him, but it was hard for me to believe what he was saying.

"This week, Loyd," John instructed, "I want you to have a conversation with that part of you that is suffering. I want you to sit in a chair." He stood up, and picked up a chair, and placed it in front of me. "I want you to sit in a chair and say what you have to say to the suffering part of you. And then I want you to get up and sit in the other chair," indicating the chair he had placed in front of me, "and as the suffering part of you, respond to what you have just told it. Go back and forth, moving from chair to chair, and get out all you have to say to each other. I think you will learn a lot. Take notes afterward in your journal."

Still standing, John went on. "Ken, you are going to practice containing your companion when it appears." Walking over to the door, he signaled the end of our first session. "I look forward to seeing you in a few days. In the meantime, be tender with each other. You are doing great work."

The ride home was much the same as the ride to Knoxville, quiet. I was grateful to have John in my life and to work with a foundation that gives Ken and me the time to be able to see him so often. Grateful or not, I found myself feeling hurt. Ken's openness and honesty were hard to hear. I wanted the truth; whether I liked it or not was neither here nor there. It just wasn't easy.

Ken must have felt my hurt in the silence. He pulled off the road at a rest area and shared his concern of his honesty hurting me. He reached for me and I rested in his arms. I, in turn, shared my gratitude that he was even aware it could be hurtful to me. Both of us felt relieved and shaky. We had begun the work of mending our lives and of trusting in John's ability to lead us through the minefields.

28.

Face to Face with Suffering

There appears to be a thin line between suffering and grief. Suffering is 'wallowing' in my feelings, unconsciously believing it will make me feel better. It was as John had said, an indulgence—an unnecessary add-on to my grief. I must have been enjoying it in some way since I was doing so much of it. But truthfully, it didn't make me feel better. I felt much, much worse.

When I was suffering, my thinking was twisted, convoluted—weird. For instance, in the homework John had assigned me, I was shocked to hear my Self say to my Suffering Self, "Because of his behavior, Ken has to experience my suffering—my pain—otherwise he gets off easy, like this was no big deal. I suffer and he suffers because I suffer. It's like a form of punishment. The more I suffer, the more he is punished. Is this crazy or what?

For some odd reason, I had the expectation that therapy would remove any depression I might feel in the coming months. I also thought the work at hand might be hard, but we would move through it relatively easily and, of course, with a minimum of pain. I see the absurdity now, but then it made perfectly good sense. As they say, "Denial is more than a river in Egypt." Clearly, I did not have much experience with depression nor had I had any long-term experience with therapy.

In reality there were days I could hardly get out of bed, days of hard heart-and-soul work. Many times I did not see the point of it all and would have liked to give it all up. The deeper I went into my pain, the farther it appeared I needed to go. My sweet, innocent, trusting self was dead, and I mourned her loss. Despair and anger seemed to be crowding me out and occupying my body like an alien being.

It was time for me to do my homework.

I did as John had directed and got out of my seat into the chair I had put in front of me and sat down. Immediately my Suffering Self matter-of-factly asked, "How are you going to be in touch with your feelings without me?"

Moving back to my seat, my Self replied, "I was feeling my feelings fine before you came along. But I have to say, conjuring you up makes me feel better in a weird, self-righteous way. I *have* been wronged. I am using you to punish Ken...." The light bulb went off in my head "AND my Self! Good grief, I don't have to punish either one of us!! Why do you want me to suffer?"

Up again to the other chair, my Suffering Self crowed, "I want you to suffer because it stops you from dealing fully with what happened in your relationship. And you deserve to suffer. After all, it was your fault."

I was aware when I moved into the chair and spoke as my Suffering Self, my whole body leaned forward as if to get in my face. I would also pick up my foot as I spoke and put it on the seat of my Self. What a gesture. Not only was the Suffering Self in my face but holding my body down with a foot! Boy, if Freud ever got hold of my journal, he would have me certified!

Back in my seat, I marveled at the strange logic of my Suffering Self. For twenty or thirty minutes, we talked.

Toward the end, my Self said, "I *want* to deal with my relationship and all that has happened. I don't want to go through this again. I also want you to stop torturing me and keeping me in pain. Stop it! When images come into my mind I will tell you to stop it. Over and over again, if I have to."

I moved back into the chair. Agreeably, my Suffering Self sweetly said, "I hear you. I'll stop now and if I do it again, you will ask me to stop, again."

Startled at the sudden willingness of my Suffering Self, I remembered the line from the Bible when the devil was tempting Jesus in the desert—"the devil departed, biding his time" (Luke 4:13). I realized I needed to be on my guard. My Suffering Self would "bide her time" and could easily slip in and become a driving force in my life.

John is a genius. When he gave me "homework," it helped just knowing there was something I *could* do. Of course, I had put this exercise off thinking it would be too painful, but it was helpful and not as hard as I thought. It helped remove some of the helpless, hopeless feelings I had.

29.

All Manner of Thing Shall Be Well

Days passed into weeks with the regularity of how life is. Spring was finally poking its green head up through the layers of leaves. Looking out the windows, I could see the pale green of new beginnings creeping up the distant mountains, softening the view.

Life was still in turmoil but with a twist of normalcy to it. I kept reminding myself I would get through this. Daily I prayerfully read the words I had written in the front of my journal attributed to the fifteenth century mystic, Julian of Norwich. "All shall be well, and all shall be well, and all manner of thing [sic] shall be well." It was said these were her last words before she died. They were a comforting mantra to me in my moments of feeling near death.

I was near death.

It was time for the old me—the old ways of being—the old ways of relating to Ken, my children, and my world—to die. It was a sure if sometimes shaky death, but it was needed. I have heard some describe it as peeling away the layers of an onion. For me it was more like using a chisel and chip, chip, chip—not a whole lot of fun—labor-intensive, loaded with tears and lots of blisters.

Lots of blisters for Ken as well. He had been amazingly strong and, at the same time, tender. I think he was a good definition of courage, for he had the strength to stand tall in the face of all my fits of fury and was willing to hold me through my struggle and his own. It was inspirational. "All shall be well."

30.

The Source of My Suffering

The drives to and from Knoxville twice a week continued. The road and landmarks became embedded in my mind. I knew, for instance, when we passed under a certain bridge on I-40 it would take us exactly 45 minutes to reach John's door. And no one could have told me Buddy's Bar-B-Q with a Buddy's chocolate shake would turn into my favorite comfort food.

Work with John was going well but, God, it was hard.

In one session we spent a great deal of time talking about Jane. She was often actively involved in my thoughts and fears. I wondered how Ken really felt about her now. Was the affair really over or was he having regrets? Did he think about her? Was he secretly wishing he could be with her? At times I felt so hurt and angry I feared he would much rather be with her than me. I could hardly stand to be with me; how could he?

I nervously shared my thoughts and questions out loud to John. He looked at me, shrugged, and gestured toward Ken, "He's the one to ask, not me."

I felt my face getting red. It was hard facing Ken and repeating my questions. I wanted to know his answers, but I hated asking. I wanted to be reassured. He was supposed to give me the answers without my asking. I thought I would know the answers by the way he acted toward me. Maybe it's a girl thing. It just boiled down to—I didn't want to ask for assurance. I wanted Ken to know he needed to reassure me a lot and to do it a lot!

Ken listened patiently to my questions and my ramblings. When I was finished, he began to answer my concerns. "After I decided to stay and work on our marriage, I felt pretty numb towards Jane the first two or three weeks. I felt relieved to have it over and to be done with all the secrecy. I was and still am very grateful you didn't throw me out of the house. And I have absolutely no regrets about ending the affair—not a one. You are who I want to be with."

He turned and looked at John. "I think being numb was an act of grace so I could separate from Jane." Turning back to me he, added, "I've had images of her since then, but I found it easy to let them go—thankfully it hasn't been the plague it's been in the past."

John spoke up, "Why is that?"

"I think it's because of the 'cabin in Maine' you gave me to practice. It works! Even the first time I tried it, it worked," Ken replied.

"My homework worked for me as well," I said.

I described the conversation with my Suffering Self, the gestures, and the body language.

John excitedly asked, "Show me how your body felt when you began the conversation. Sculpt it for me."

I bent over in my chair almost in a fetal position.

John jumped out of his chair, came over to me, and put his hands on my back, pushing me into an even tighter fetal position. "So here's your Suffering Self leaning on you, bending you over, weighing you down."

He pushed harder. I was having trouble breathing, John is a big man!

I gasped for breath and he said, "So who is doing all this, Loyd? Who is causing you all this suffering? Who is making it tough for you to get your breath?"

"Me," I managed to squeeze out of my throat. "It's me."

John let go and stepped back. "You betcha!" he grinned, clapping his hands when he sat back down. "And who can put a stop to it?"

Grinning back, I replied meekly, "Me."

31.

Hearing My Own Voice

One of John's favorite exercises with us was to put that infamous chair in front of one of us and have us talk out loud to the invisible person sitting there. If I was angry with that person sitting in the chair, I was to tell her so in great detail. No holds barred. This was not done in a quiet tone of voice as though we were sitting on a bus together. No such luck. *All* I had to say was said with all the fury I felt inside of me.

I discovered having conversations with people who aren't there was sometimes harder than talking face to face. I think it was hearing my own voice that got to me. Shouting in someone's office plus being observed doesn't help either. And then there were the horrible things that came out of my mouth.

I'll admit it, I did not like this exercise. Intellectually I understood the purpose of doing it. I agreed it was healthy to get all the negative thoughts and feelings out of my body. I still believe it was important to do. But in front of John and Ken and in John's office with people walking around outside his door? Nope, it was awkward and I felt embarrassed.

Being raised to be a Southern lady is a blessing and a curse. You do not raise your voice in anger nor tell another what is making you angry. Well, you can sometimes tell them you are angry, but you never tell them "in great detail." Mostly you show your anger by your huffiness or coldness—we all have our favorite ways of letting the other person know. But out loud, to his face? It's just not done. Even if you are thinking "in great detail."

Instead, anger was handled by burying it—stuffing it deep inside. In time you learned to ignore the pain in your gut or the uneasiness. The anger might leak out occasionally as hostility or an out-of-proportion fury about something as mundane as who didn't feed the dog. But, as Miss Scarlett would say, "Fiddle-de-dee"; you could worry about that tomorrow.

Burying, stuffing, denying, overriding my feelings, pretending, justifying— all were useless. Resentment had set in no matter what good reasons I had. A deadly killer was lurking in my heart and soul. And the worst part was I knew it. With cold, or sometimes hot, calculating precision, the data of each upset were stored "in great detail" in my mind. The ledger was kept and sealed in wax with a self-righteous stamp that read, "It was their fault."

John urged me to go for it, get out my anger, speak what was true for me, and "unhook my spirit," as Caroline Myss, the author of *The Anatomy of the Spirit,* says.

I was way out of my comfort zone. I tucked my hands under my thighs and held on for dear life. With eyes closed and all the breath I could suck in, I took a giant step toward freedom with the first words I called out from the bottom of my rage. I yelled to the invisible Jane, "Daaaaamn yooou!"

From then on out rolled every piece of garbage large and small I had believed about this woman—"in great detail."

What did I learn from this seemingly simple exercise? I woke up to the amazing realization that Jane was not sitting in that chair for just herself and her behavior. She was representing much more. She had the face of every woman I had ever known who had betrayed me, hurt me, called me friend, and abused my caring for her. Even more startling, she also wore my face. Mine.

97

32.

A Grace-Filled Birthday

Happy birthday to me. I chose an ANGEL® Card this morning, wanting an angel to be with me for the coming year. Her name is "Grace." I looked up the meaning for my angel Grace and, of course, was struck by how perfect she is for me right now. "Grace—poise and elegance in form, attitude, and action. Give up the struggle and allow the universe to participate in the creation of your life." Thank you, universe, for taking such good care of me and giving Grace to me as my birthday present. May I gracefully let go and receive all the gifts you have to offer me this year.

I didn't feel much like going out to dinner for my birthday, so Ken surprised me. He set the dining room table with the silver and best china and in the center of the table he placed beautiful fresh flowers. It was lovely. Ken was totally out of his element in this, and it was touching seeing him scurrying around, going to great efforts to make this a special event.

Ken isn't a cook, so I couldn't imagine what he had concocted for dinner.

"Close your eyes," he ordered.

Leading me into the dining room, he again admonished me to keep my eyes closed. Sitting me in my chair, he put my napkin in my lap, I heard him light the candles, and off he went into the kitchen.

I listened for the banging of pots and pans. Nothing. I was really getting curious. In a matter of minutes he was back again. "Now open your eyes." With a great flourish he served me my plate. I had an incredible slice of rare roast beef, a baked potato with sour cream, barely steamed asparagus, and a salad—absolutely delicious. He had worked hard on the presentation of it all, and it was impeccable—all ordered from a local restaurant. Smart man! Thankfully Ken didn't order a birthday cake with fifty-seven candles to light on it. It would have looked like an inferno and probably would have set off the smoke detector.

I was warmed by his love, touched by his earnestness, and grateful for his thoughtfulness. It had been a long time since I had felt this way towards him.

Earlier that day I was thinking about my age, and I caught myself looking down at my hands. They looked like Mother's. I look so much like her I am sometimes startled when I look in the mirror. We moved here not long after she died, and I am sad she didn't live long enough to experience Mariposa. I miss her.

She would have loved this place, the wild flowers, the birds, and Dickens and Clio. I sometimes see her when I walk with the dogs. She walks alongside me pointing out flowers, weeds, and tall grass, whatever would be interesting to dry and put in a floral arrangement. "Old dry," she called the dried material she picked from the roadsides. She'd get arrested now. I can see her laughing at the prospect.

Sometimes when you walked into Mother's bedroom, you would have to weave through stacks of magazines in various spots piled on top of the rug. The uneducated observer might have thought she was turning into one of the crazy Collier brothers, who never threw anything away, stacking and saving all those magazines, but the rest of us knew why they were there. She was flattening and drying "old dry" for her next arrangement.

"To Mother," I said as I lifted my wine glass. "To you and to Daddy." I thanked them for bringing me into this world and, all things considered, for doing a very good job of parenting me. Happy birthday to me.

33.

So Much for Fear

I can feel myself shut down when Ken's voice gets that tone of patient irritation. If it turns into a tirade, I automatically snarl back all my answers, defending myself left and right. I yell back at him saying words to hurt, all the time feeling fearful and to blame. My fear convinces me I am at fault. Why else would he have reason to be angry and yell at me? If he gets out of control, hyper, I keep a calm exterior, but I can feel the color leave my face and inside me there is chaos.

I think his enthusiasm or excitement gets to me when I perceive it is "out of control" and, of course, I get to judge when it is out of control. Ken asked me to tell him what I liked about his excitement. When I described it, he said my words sounded "contained" and they did. I told him it was his "aliveness" I liked and when it got loud and exaggerated, I didn't like it. I used the example of a mutual friend, who when his enthusiasm is all over the place, Ken has expressed how he doesn't like it, and feels irritated and impatient when he spends time with him. When our friend isn't all over the place, Ken feels very different—warm and relaxed, and enjoys his company. He understood what I meant.

Ken wants me to tell him when his excitement is all over the place and how I am feeling. I've tried that before, but we are in a very different place and perhaps he can hear me now. There is also something important to recognize here. We have never talked about any of this. Mostly we have reacted and never gone into the why of it. That in itself changes everything.

Enthusiasm. *The Merriam-Webster Dictionary* defines "enthusiasm" as: to be inspired. 1: strong warmth of feeling: keen interest: fervor 2: a cause of fervor.

Sounds relatively benign in the reading of it. It surely didn't feel benign in our session with John. Ken did most of the talking. Specifically, he was talking about when he is enthusiastic about something. In those moments he experiences himself as centered, connected to the people he is with, engaging those around him into whatever he is excited about, powerful, enthusiastic!

John asked me, "When Ken is enthusiastic, do you experience him as he described it?"

I sighed. "Rarely. If he gets really excited about something, sometimes he becomes scattered—he is all over the place—hyperactive. There is no calming him down. At those times I feel frightened—not safe. I feel like I am being rolled over by an out-of-control Mack truck."

"Loyd, those are your judgments of the power he is expressing," John said. "Tell me about this power without your negative judgment. Describe it to me."

Struggling to think differently and to find the words, I said, "Excited, focused, going for it. This isn't easy."

"Tell me more."

"Wanting you to know everything, motivated. Passionate comes to my mind."

"When you take your judgments off of it, it sounds like someone you would want to be around, doesn't it?"

"Yes," I admitted. "I can see the difference."

John turned to Ken. "Did Jane see your enthusiasm?"

"Yes," Ken answered.

BEYOND THE AFFAIR

"And how was she with it?"

Ken's eyes brightened. "She loved it!" Ken replied.

If you had taken a baseball bat and hit me in my solar plexus, I don't think I could have been more stunned. I thought my heart would break. The whole room felt like it had moved, tilted.

I was furious. "I would cut off my right arm for you to have focused all that attention, passion, enthusiasm, or whatever else you want to call it on me," I sobbed. Gasping for breath, I continued, "I have even asked for it and you chose to give it to her. You said that you 'gave up on me' when you never tried; you went looking elsewhere."

John gently said, "Loyd, can you see how if you're judging enthusiasm as scattered and scary, Ken might take it elsewhere?"

I nodded, feeling torn to pieces. I said to myself, "So this is one of my contributions that made it easy for him to go elsewhere. My reaction and judgments about his enthusiasm are a part of why all this happened."

I felt sick and heavy with grief. A profound realization filled my mind and spilled out of my mouth, "It isn't just Ken's affair, is it? It is our affair."

The words, "our affair," permeated the room like the scent of strong-smelling flowers—unavoidable in their presence.

"Loyd," John said, "you're right. It is very important that you both understand the affair is about the both of you—it took the two of you. It is, as you said, 'our affair.' Good for you for putting that together. However," he said pointing his finger at me, "do not take on Ken's decision to behave as he did. That is *not* your part. It was his decision. You did not make him decide to have an affair. Do you hear that? He decided to do what he did. You contributed, yes, but he did not have to decide to have an affair. He had other choices."

I listened intently, doing my best to absorb what John was saying. I felt like I was peering through a fog. My mind was close to being overwhelmed, and I was reaching for any life-preserving words I could hear to keep me from drowning in my sea of awareness.

There was not much conversation on the way back home. Both of us were engrossed in our own thoughts. It had been a powerful and painful session. I sensed we had walked through the shallows into the deeper waters of our therapy. Though I knew this was good and where we needed to go, it still felt threatening and scary. The old way of relating wasn't too sure of what the new way of relating was going to look like—and, the big question was could I move from the old to the new? And did I even want to continue with our marriage?

When I surfaced out of my thoughts, I could see we were driving through one of the prettiest sections of our route home. Down below us on the right water cascaded over rocks and flowed between ancient mountain laurels. Above and on both sides of the road loomed the mountains. Their high peaks almost blocked out the light of the sun now low in the sky.

We would be home before dark, but just barely. I could imagine there would be two very excited Jack Russell terriers waiting for our arrival. With a deep breath I reassured myself that I was fine, *all shall be well.* I spent the rest of the journey doing my best to let the healing energy of the surrounding mountains bolster my sagging spirits.

34.

Done In

Once we arrived home, Ken dashed off to a board meeting, and I settled down with the dogs. Clio curled up next to me obviously glad for my return. Dickens let me know that his preference was to go for a walk in the dark. However, he jumped up on the sofa and stretched out on the other side of me. Resting his head on my thigh, he looked up at me as only he could do and let me know that because it was me, he would forgo the walk. Such a sacrifice.

By the time Ken arrived home from his meeting, I was not doing too well. In spite of everything I had tried to do, I could not let go of some of the things that were said at John's. Particularly, "*She* loved it!" I felt completely done-in— whipped to the bone.

Ken listened to my pain. "As soon as I heard myself say, 'She loved it' with the tone and energy I had behind it, I knew what your reaction would be. I was really angry at John for even asking me the question. I want you to know, Jane never experienced what you call my 'Mack truck' enthusiasm—who knows, it might have scared her too."

"I don't want to be scared," I retorted, "I want to 'love it.' Maybe when we do John's assignment and dialogue about your enthusiasm, I'll understand what happens to me."

We talked for awhile longer, sharing the thoughts we had been thinking on our ride home. It was relieving and becoming more comfortable to talk to each other. I so appreciated Ken's participation. I had no sense of his holding back and felt loved and accepted and full of hope. What a move from how I had felt earlier.

The next day we did the exercise John suggested and dialogued about Ken's enthusiasm. It seems so silly now, but I felt the anxiety of the unknown begin to creep into my body as well as my mind. I was afraid Ken would use the exercise as an opportunity to dump his anger on me. He hadn't used any of the exercises we'd done as an excuse to blow up at me, but I think there were times when I felt so vulnerable and unable to cope with much of anything, I automatically thought I was going to "get got!" Poor Ken, I laid so much on him. Actually, in the back of my mind, I had to admit I believed it *was* wrong of me to think his enthusiasm, scattered or not, wasn't wonderful; perhaps I was deserving of his anger. After all, Jane loved it.

We talked back and forth for some time. Neither one of us was angry nor was it a particularly hard exercise. My fears can magnify anything into a horrific happening. Why didn't I give up being afraid? What was it that kept my fears in place? Holding on to them always ended up being a huge waste of my time, not to mention my energy.

Interestingly, we discovered in the course of the exercise that Ken's excitement and passion for life and his various pursuits do not frighten me at all. What I feared and what I labeled as enthusiasm wasn't enthusiasm at all. My fear would rise up when he became hyperactive—when he talked as though adrenaline had kicked in and he got loud and repetitive. I also sensed an undercurrent of anger or hostility when all this was happening. All I wanted to do then was back away from him and not listen to anything he had to say.

This, we agreed, was not enthusiasm. Although these times were not frequent, I had somehow lumped the enthusiasm I enjoy with this other behavior and condemned them both, leaving Ken no place to go with either.

35.

My Job

As I went to bed, I thought again about what I heard Sharon Daloz Parks say at a seminar I went to this morning. It struck a deep chord within me. She spoke about a couple and their suffering—the pain and trauma in their relationship. She said they loved, and loved, and loved, and painful events happened in their relationship anyway. What she called "shipwrecks" happen in our life—often with the repercussions of deep grief and pain so ravaging that death would be welcomed. Whew! Did that sound familiar.

I had a hard time controlling myself as I sat in the auditorium listening to her. My tears wanted to give in to sobs and childlike shuddering. Sharon had to have said "deep grief" at least three times and each time it went down into the core of me. She also read a poem, which didn't help my tears either. After her lecture I was unable to stay and chitchat with friends. I just wanted to come back home to my refuge. Her words pretty well filled my afternoon and night.

Somehow, in something Sharon said, I felt free to accept my grief. A "shipwreck" had occurred, and it was okay for me to grieve. It was my job right now. But—and here's the rub—if there is grief, something has died. What has died—innocence, our marriage, trust in Ken, trust in God, confidence in myself, my love? I am afraid our marriage is dead and all the above as well. Death is pretty damn permanent! I do think the old way of living out our marriage is dead. The trust, confidence, love must have died too. I don't like writing this down. I know there can be resurrection, but, again, do I want to build a new way? Some days no, some days yes. I feel tired just thinking about it.

Ken and I were enjoying our morning tea. We had read the paper and were spending some time talking about how we were going to spend the day.

Putting his cup down, he turned to me and said, "I have had a light bulb go off about how I have been relating to you."

My stomach flopped. I dreaded what he might say.

He reached over and touched my hand. "I think you are a genius."

Shocked, I incredulously repeated, "You think I am a genius? Where in the world did that come from?"

"Yes, I do, and I think I have believed it forever. I have always thought you worked better with people than I. Particularly in our job with the foundation of talking on the phone encouraging people to teach courses. You seem to tap into their issues of why they are struggling or not keeping their intentions of what they want to do." He smiled, "You say things to them that amaze me—things I would never have thought of. And, to make matters worse, you are exceptionally creative. There is 'genius' about you."

As I listened, my first thoughts were to point out how he does the same thing just differently from me. I am aware I can "connect the dots" of what people are saying quickly and can help them see things in a different light—but genius? I started to protest, but he obviously wasn't finished, so for a change I sat quietly.

"The light bulb was realizing I believe I am *not* a genius. Therefore, I have to keep you from discovering you are—hence my competitiveness with you, though you rarely play the game of competing along with me."

"What do you mean? What do you think you do to keep me from this discovery?"

"Let me think a minute."

He gazed out the window at the birds flocking to the bird feeder. My heart was warmed by the look of concentration on his face. I realized how much I loved the dimple in his chin and his intensity as he worked at explaining himself. I thought, love was not dead, just hidden behind my fears and anger at times.

Pulling himself back to me, he said, "Well, for instance, you know how I always wanted you to go to college? Yes, I know, it was more of a demand than a want. It wasn't high on your list of things to do and I couldn't understand that. But when I was working with the insurance company in Ohio and you were here in North Carolina, you decided to take a course at UNCA. You were having a great experience—writing papers, class discussions. Every phone call we had during that time was full of what fun you were having because of this class."

I nodded in agreement.

"So what did I do? I wanted you to leave and come to Ohio because I was so lonely. I was miserable and I insisted. I remember talking long and hard to convince you to come."

"Yes, I remember it too. I didn't want to quit, but you convinced me." Laughing, I said, "It took everything I had to screw up my courage and talk with my professor and ask him to write a letter giving me permission to withdraw. I didn't want to have an F on my record!"

Ken reached over and picked up my hand. Holding it between his hands, he said, "I think it was an unconscious way of keeping you down and unaware of your ability. Even though my loneliness was intense, I could have waited until you had completed the quarter. I know it wasn't a conscious thing; I was totally unaware of this dynamic until now."

Tears welled up in his eyes as he continued, "I unconsciously didn't want you to know how bright you are. I am sure I have done a lot of things like that in order for me to look better than you. I want you to know I am so sorry. College or no college, you have it all over me."

Listening in amazement and seeing his obvious sadness, I found myself struggling to keep from correcting him. I was not a genius nor did I have it all over him. How could he think such a thing?

One more time I found myself slipping into an old belief. Of course I couldn't take in the possibility that Ken could think of me as a genius—"bright" I could hear, but not "genius"—that was too impossible. The old belief of Loyd—you are fundamentally stupid—rose up and screamed at me. I was so convinced I was stupid for so long that years ago I had myself tested by a psychologist just to prove how stupid I was! My friends couldn't believe I would go that far when all the evidence proved otherwise. The testing proved I was no genius but was in the top 2.5 percentile in intelligence.

Evidence or not, all I could tell myself was, if you are a genius, you would not be in this mess. I would have seen Ken distancing himself from me. And I certainly would have picked up the first lie that left his lips.

To my credit, I didn't try to convince Ken he had it all wrong. It was enough that he shared his realization with me—his honesty and his apology.

36.

Panic

Feelings of terror woke me at 3 a.m. My mind was going crazy, and I decided to get up and write. I awoke thinking, when September arrives, we will mutually decide to stay together or divorce. Ken can say, "I'm out of here." I hadn't really taken that in. I'm the wronged party here—I'll decide! All this time I had been thinking I would make the decision. What did I think "mutually decide" meant? This scares me big time.

He could be doing his thing and slyly planning to leave—could really set me up. He looked right in my eyes for three months and lied to me, and he could still be lying to me. Maybe he wouldn't go back to Jane, but he would have "done his time" with me. He could take me for everything—the house, the dogs, property, money—and I'd be left with nothing. At the beginning of all of this, he told me he'd divorce me and be fair. I am to believe that?

Should I gather evidence to protect myself? I have my journal. Is that enough documentation? He destroyed the cellular phone bills for the last three months, so they're gone. What else could be evidence? Should I photocopy his journal? I am stunned I am even thinking this. But am I being lulled into not taking care of myself?

I hate this. I am afraid to trust him. How do I know he is telling me the truth? And why am I so afraid he will leave me? If he is still lying to me, I wouldn't want to be with him.

Having all this stuff sitting in my head isn't going to help our relationship. I know I can't keep this to myself. We agreed not to keep secrets. Of course, I was thinking I had no secrets. My, how things are getting refined. Realistically, holding onto these beliefs and keeping all this to myself is a definite secret, plus it is a seed bed for resentments. So much for Miss Goodie-Two-Shoes.

Two months had passed since the confrontation at the kitchen table. It felt more like two years. Every day, practically every moment, had been chock full of lessons, fears, and every other emotion. It was at times exhausting and at other times exhilarating.

I still had not moved far from my concerns of Ken leaving me. In my thinking, I should have been beyond that. After all he was still with me. What was my problem? I had moments of realization, middle-of-the-night musings, times in which I scared myself with possibilities.

At breakfast, I shared my middle-of-the-night fears. Ken sat quietly stroking Dickens, listening intently to all I had to say, nodding occasionally.

When I had finished, he rose up from the table and said, "I am going to take my shower."

"I am going to take my shower" wasn't the response I was expecting. I watched him head toward the bathroom. With irritation in my voice, I said, "Ken, it would help me to hear what you are thinking other than you want to take your shower."

He stopped, turned around, and walked slowly towards me. When he reached the table, he bent his head over and placed both hands on the table. I could feel my heart beating. Dickens raised his head and we both felt the silence. What *was* he thinking?

With his hands still on the table he straightened his head, looked into my waiting eyes, and said, "I have said this to you before and I guess you keep needing to hear it again. Loyd, I love you, I really do and I *have* decided never to leave you. I want to spend the rest of my life creating a rich fulfilling life for us—together."

I began to cry.

He came around the table and sat down on the window seat next to me. Wiping my tears, he said, "I know I destroyed your trust, and I know it will take time to rebuild. I find myself feeling tired of repeating myself and wishing all of this was over and you no longer were worried. But it isn't over. It will just take time and I am here for all time."

I sat there soaking up his words into my parched heart. "This is so hard," I said. "When I share my feelings and what I am thinking, I think it is one way of rebuilding trust—not keeping secrets from you and you from me. But then I get worried that if I do share, I will drive you away. Hearing you say you are tired of hearing me confirms it."

Pulling me to him, he whispered, "You can't drive me away and I didn't say I was tired of hearing you. I am not leaving—period. I don't know how to say it any plainer."

We held each other, and I began to feel some relief and gratitude for Ken's patience. It is so easy for me to read things into everything he says. Truly not fair I seemed to be looking at him only through eyes of suspicion. No one can be constantly scrutinized and pass with flying colors. It would help if I could lighten up.

Truthfully, I think Ken was telling me the truth and I found it hard to believe him. I was so trusting in the past, I never even thought about it. It would be easy for me to do the very thing he had done and keep secrets, believing it somehow would have kept me from getting hurt. It was a choice I made—to share my feelings even when they were scary and to tell him what I wanted. Good for me and good for us!

I spent years of needing no particular reminders of Ken's love. I knew my love was there for him, and I believed he felt like I did. He often told me he oved me, hugged me, and I the same. Now I felt so "needy." I didn't like it. It smacked of a clinging vine that weighed down the one it wrapped itself around until eventually the object of the vine's affections died of strangulation. Grim. I didn't want to be a clinging vine.

The sound of Ken showering kept me company as I stared out the window. Clio and Dickens had found just the right spot of sun on the deck. Oh, for the life of a dog or at least one of our dogs. Just looking at them brought on a smile. They had stretched out their little bodies to take full advantage of the warmth of both the deck and the sun—the ultimate in contentment. I imagined their minds empty of worry, not the least bit concerned about where their next meal would come from or whether they were loved or not. Would that I could adopt their way of being, their "doggie-ness". Instead, I got caught up in my fears. It was time to drop these thoughts—find the sun in my life for a change.

37.

Disarming Conflict

I have always struggled with fights and arguments. In my youth, "raised" voices" were not permitted. I was brought up in the era of "children were to be seen and not heard." Unknowingly, I think my parents believed it meant adults as well. If my parents fought, it was very quietly.

There was no doubt when Daddy was irritated; it oozed out of his pores. My sister and I would pick up the scent and "lay low"—Southern for "don't rock the boat." He huffed and puffed—but, of course, quietly. When Mother was upset, it was obvious too. Ann and I knew to watch out when her curving lips would vanish into a straight line. And guess what? My lips do the same when I get upset!

I remember hearing a confrontation only once in my house. I was about ten years old. Ann had broken one of the cardinal rules of the house. She had not called home to let Mother and Daddy know she was going somewhere else after she had arrived at her original destination.

I couldn't understand why everyone was so upset. Mother, Daddy, and Ann met upstairs in Ann's room. I was not invited. Daddy hammered her with questions and lectured her about I don't know what, but I know the sounds of one of his lectures when I hear it. I never heard Mother's voice—only Ann and Daddy. To my young ears, it sounded like the Spanish Inquisition—unfair, loud, hurtful, and scary. (Need I tell you, I never forgot to call and let them know where I was?)

"Avoid conflict whenever possible" was my rule of thumb. If you can't avoid it, grin and bear it or—even better—ignore it and it will go away. Right? Wrong.

In John's office I discovered there are other ways of dealing with conflict. What an eye-opening experience.

Part of what I learned was that in a relationship conflict is a given. That was a huge surprise for me. The reality that conflict is—it just is—was mind-boggling for me. It broke the myriad of myths I grew up believing, such as conflict is all bad; nothing good can come from conflict; if there is conflict, something is wrong with me/Ken/the relationship; happy people aren't in conflict; someone must win, someone—me—must lose.

It never occurred to me that conflict was a natural occurrence when two or more people work at relating to each other. Why is that? Simplistically speaking, we are different from each other.

Let's face it, Ken has had his life experiences growing up with his parents, being with his friends, attending various schools, being in business, and I have had mine. We brought all those experiences into our marriage. They were not alike—similar, but not the same. This is the kicker—even when we experience the same thing, we experience it differently simply because we are different from each other. Consequently, we all will have our differences and will be in conflict from time to time.

Amazing. It made such sense. It is not a perfect world, goodness knows I know that, but my expectation had been that Ken and I would somehow avoid conflict just by loving each other. If we were upset with each other, something must be terribly wrong. If all was right, there would be no conflict. I had unconsciously bought the fairy tale lie, "and they lived happily ever after, forever and ever." With all of my knowledge, I had been living in the Dark Ages.

BEYOND THE AFFAIR

The other piece of my new learning was that conflict can be a powerful opportunity for two people to grow together. Conflict need not split people apart. Though I didn't know what our decision would be in September, I felt closer to Ken than I had ever felt.

38.

Decibel Levels

John worked hard with us on various techniques of communicating. Obviously, one of the hardest communications for me was when Ken became angry with me and shouted. The decibel level was more than I could stand, and I wanted to cover my ears and disappear. "Loud" was the operative word. Loud and repetitious. It works best for Ken to make his complaint six or seven times. Saying something one or two times won't do it. I have thought he must become enamored of the sound of his voice.

"John, what do I do when Ken is angry and starts yelling?" I asked with hope for some answers.

"What do you think your options are?" asked John. Smiling, he picked up his trusty magic marker, clearly preparing to expand my possibilities.

"Ignore him, cover my ears, yell back at him," I responded.

John got up and went to the newsprint. "Ignoring him is a little hard. Covering your ears doesn't work, but yelling back at him has real possibilities."

Puzzled, I said, "I don't want to participate in a yelling contest."

Having drawn two unflattering stick figures on the newsprint, John turned and looked at me. "What do you suppose would happen if you matched his volume?" Turning back to the newsprint, he began to write what he was saying, "If he's talking in a normal tone, match it. If he gets louder, match it. If he gets even louder, match that loudness as well. What do you think will happen?"

I laughed and said, "Dickens and Clio will leave the room."

Ken chimed in, "I think if she matched the volume of what I said, it might have an effect on how long I was willing to yell. She'd be yelling back at me and it would cease to be fun."

Shocked, I said, "Fun! You have to be kidding—yelling at me is fun to you?"

John moved to the center of the room and motioned for the two of us to join him. "Here's the scenario. Loyd, you're Ken's neighbor and your dog has just dug up Ken's freshly planted garden. He is not happy. Ken, I want you to knock on her door and tell her in no uncertain terms what you think about her dog, what kind of neighbor she is for letting her dog loose, and whatever else comes into your angry mind. Then, Loyd, I want you to reply to him matching his volume. I am going to stand behind you so Ken can see me and you can't. Ken, watch me raise and lower my hand as I signal to you whether to talk quietly or loudly." Stepping behind me he repeated, "Remember Loyd, match his volume. Got it?"

We nodded and began. As we talked, John signaled Ken and softly at first, then loudly, up and down we went. I felt stupid at the beginning, and the louder we got the more uncomfortable I became. I had visions of the other therapists and clients in the building wondering what in the world was going on with the crazy clients in John's office.

We stopped to get our breath and I nervously said, "I wonder what the people in the rest of the office are thinking."

With his hands on his hips, John admonished, "Loyd, let go of what others think. Just do it."

So on we went. I got to the point where I was totally in it and forgot who else might be listening, a big step for me. I did have a booming headache, which was a sure sign of my uptightness. But I did it.

After a few rounds of practicing, John asked, "Well, what do you think?"

Ken laughed and said, "I think it might help me to stop yelling at Loyd."

John grinned, "Why would it stop you?"

"Because I don't like hearing how loud I sound. If she matches the volume, I can't miss my loudness."

I replied, "Well, that's good news. When you hear me echoing you, you are actually experiencing what I experience. I love it that you don't like it either."

John said, "Good observation. Now I want you to try something else. This time I want you to talk at the same time and I'll conduct the volume again."

Good grief! Back to the salt mines. We sounded even worse than before. Not only were we loud, but it sounded like we were having a free-for-all of words.

After we sat down, we both remarked how we could completely understand what the other was saying even though we were talking at the same time. I never would have thought it possible—our brains are remarkable.

John said, "It really is amazing even though you are both talking at the same time, you don't miss a thing of what either of you is saying. Nothing is lost. I want you two to practice both exercises at least three times before you come back. Also, Loyd, something for you to consider—when Ken gets angry, if neither of these exercises is working for you, you can always choose to leave the room."

"Wow, that's a novel concept!" I responded.

"So, well done, you two," John praised as he walked to the door. "Next session I want to focus on some of the conflicts around Jane."

What an end to the session. Certainly I had plenty of conflict with Jane, but what did John have in mind—worry, worry.

39.

Feeling Sick Isn't Healthy

Lately I had been having long, detailed conversations in my head with Jane, so much so they were getting in my way. John's suggestion of doing a conflict exercise only added to an already steady stream of inner talk.

It was a warm Sunday afternoon. The door to the deck was open, and smells of spring wafted through the cabin. Debbie, a close friend, had come up the mountain for a leisurely visit. Leisurely wasn't her usual mode of operation. Anyone who knows Debbie knows she is a fireball. For her to stop and be with us was a gift and I was grateful for her insights and her love.

In the course of our visit, I shared the frequency of my inner chatter with Jane. Debbie reminded me of the importance of getting things *out* of my head instead of having conversations stay inside me, giving them the opportunity to wreak havoc.

"If you don't want to call Jane and say what you are thinking," she said, "why don't you write her a letter?"

My whole body tightened as I looked over at Ken. "Ken suggested the same thing."

Debbie sat up in her chair. "Loyd, surely you don't think Ken and I are suggesting you mail it!"

We laughed.

"I know that. I don't know why, but just the thought of writing it makes me feel ill."

Debbie leaned back in her chair and said, "That's the whole idea. Get it out of your body so you won't feel ill." She suddenly looked surprised. "You know it's funny saying this to you. You have said this to me more times than I can count. Seriously, though, at some point, you need to work on forgiving Jane. Feeling sick isn't healthy. You don't need to destroy your health over all of this. And until you forgive her—" Her voice trailed off as she shrugged her shoulders.

Spoken like the nurse she is.

"I know, I know, holding on and not forgiving her will eat me up heart and soul. It *is* eating me up." Letting out a deep sigh, I said, "I can hear myself saying that to others too. I know it is important to let go, but I just can't seem to do it. I hate to say it, but I don't want to forgive her!"

Debbie got up and came over to the sofa. Sitting down next to me, she smiled and said, "I want you to know I trust you to work it out. You will know when the time is right to forgive her and you'll do it." She reached over and patted my hand. "I guess I am just so taken with how devastated you are with all of this. I don't mean it isn't tough, but I wouldn't have thought it would have thrown you so hard."

"Why do you think I am having such a hard time?" I asked.

Debbie thought a moment, "I don't know. I'll think about it and let you know if it comes to me. In the meantime, start writing. See if it doesn't help take away some of the constant conversations you're having, or at the least it might give you another outlet to vent your anger."

Ken nodded his agreement. "Two against one," I thought.

40.

The Letter

The letter was seven pages long front and back and so powerful I never had to change a line or add anything more. I had said it all. It was out and on paper. What had imprinted my heart and soul now imprinted the pages of my journal.

I was obviously ready. The only effort it took was deciding to do it. Once I began, I had no problem continuing—you might say I wasn't at a loss for words!

The process exposed my venomous thoughts ad nauseum. Again and again the anguish of betrayal stood out starkly on the white pages of my journal. The shock of secrets revealed—the lost trust—the destruction of the dream of a loving, caring husband who would do me no harm—and the absolute fury of being used by someone who called herself my friend.

Pain and grief were back out into the open like a scab knocked off a previous wound. Tears flowed and my body felt beaten down by heavy memories.

Revenge was one of the themes that ran throughout the letter—no real surprise to me. One of the dictionary definitions of revenge is "an opportunity for getting satisfaction." I wanted Jane to suffer—even die. I wanted her exposed to the world for her sexual misbehavior. Boy, did I ever want satisfaction—satisfaction that she was hurting, remorseful, grief-stricken, ashamed, repentant, and alone.

Oh, my, what a stunner. I was shocked at my own cruelty, my need to punish. It was no wonder the mere thought of writing this letter had made me feel ill. My thoughts were poisonous to my heart, soul, cells—my whole being. All the words that flowed out onto the page were close to the surface, not hidden deep inside. I didn't need a shovel or a chisel, only the pen on the page.

Though I felt some sense of relief, a quieting of my mind, I was keenly aware that an unmailed letter was not the end of my journey with Jane. Forgiveness would be the next step. I had no doubt that I would get there. The question was, when would I decide? When would I be willing to drop my feelings of revenge? When would I no longer want "satisfaction"? When would I recognize Jane's humanity as I had recognized Ken's? When would I forgive her inability to be perfect? When would I choose to heal my own heart with the balm of forgiveness?

PART III: THE BUTTERFLY

41.

Sad and Alone

We watched a television program last night which included some scenes of the slaughtering of a group of Cheyenne Indians. I broke down in sobs when survivors talked about the death of the chief's wife. They said, "All she did was care for others, want the best for others, and love her husband."

It struck me in my heart. That's me. That is what I wanted. I had wanted nothing but the best for Jane. For as long as I have known her I have done everything I knew to support and encourage her in the work she wanted to do. And I loved Ken heart and soul. I encouraged him when he was down, shared myself the best I could, and lovingly trusted him to care for me and for us.

Why did Ken give up on me? Why didn't he fight to keep me? Why wouldn't he want to love me constantly and keep reaching for me? How could he turn his back on me, throw me away as useless, not worth his efforts, and go elsewhere? Why did he do this? These questions probably have no answers I can accept.

This whole affair has shaken me down to my core. It is incredibly painful. It is almost like God is asking me to let go of everything—my trust of others, my friends, my husband, and somehow look at it all some other way.

Am I to be so confident of who I am that the rest doesn't matter? I can see the power in being secure in my own authority and who I am in the world. I could then be anywhere with anyone and be solid in myself.

Maybe it is more about letting go of the "myth" of believing that if you fully trust someone he will always do the right thing, or that everything is going to work out the way I want it. I just don't know anymore.

BEYOND THE AFFAIR

At the moment I am feeling very sad and alone.

When we went to bed, I was still awake and wanting to read. Ken wanted to sleep, and it was okay with him if I read. He crawled into bed and reached down to the foot of the bed to pick up Dickens. He rolled over on his side with his back to me curled up with Dickens. I was jealous. No touch from him for me, no "good night," no kiss, no "I love you." I felt lonely with a strange sense of being punished mixed in. Should I have turned out the light? Was he wanting something from me? After I did turn out the light, I couldn't sleep. He felt so far away from me—no reaction when I touched him, I might as well have been sleeping alone.

Freeing myself from all the hurt is taking too long. I know it has been only three months, but my body and mind feel the clock as though it were moving in slow motion. Every tick is a day and every tock a month. At times I think I am riding an emotional wave. I am out at sea, lost in the vastness, and feeling alone. The next thing I know I am at the top of a wave with shore in sight and just as quickly I am back down at the bottom of the wave out at sea again, waiting for another glimpse of land—of hope.

I have learned when life feels dark, hard, and unbearable, I can dip into the resources I have around me for support, encouragement, hope. Often these are friends, who love us both, and there is John, our therapist. Always I have unconditional love from Dickens and Clio, and sometimes I create comfort from deep inside myself.

I was grateful to have close friends with whom we were able to be open and be ourselves, warts and all. Strong friends who were quick to be with us and not take sides were a blessing. Often they told the hard truth to us. It was difficult, particularly for Ken, to hear some feedback about how comments and references he made toward and about women had been painful for others besides myself to hear. And for me to hear that it was time for me to get a handle on my own pain and move beyond it confused me.

126

Expressing my feelings was important on my road to healing. I wrote in my journal to express my feelings, but there were times I screamed and stomped, beating the chair with whatever was handy. Furiously I would let Ken know just how things were for me at the moment—sometimes when he wasn't around but, to his credit, right in his face at other times. I wept a lot, more tears than I thought were possible for one human being to shed. I had no idea anyone could be in such pain and live. Some days were tearless, but I would experience days and nights when I felt I was engulfed in a wave of pain. I learned not to fight it but to ride it instead.

Being still was on the other side of expression. Quietly resting into the center of myself with nothing but my breathing to think about helped. I was not good at this. I could often convince myself that I should be "doing" something—"being" quiet wasn't enough. But I recognized the benefits I could receive from times of quiet. Actually when I think about it, times of being still have been a lifesaver, particularly when I felt at my worst. Curling up in my chair and allowing myself to be still stopped me from running around and avoiding the hurt I was feeling. It was an opportunity to comfort myself as only I knew how to do for myself.

I think the reason some of my most creative ideas would come to me when I was in the shower was because I was still. Okay, I was bathing myself, but my mind was relatively still. I was being washed, cleansed in the process, and opened to creativity. Standing or soaking in the tub was also a powerful time for meditation. When I step into the water as a holy act of refreshment, an act of letting the water run over me and cleanse me, I receive the gift of new inspiration. Out of nowhere appear solutions or a new view of an old landscape.

I read often for understanding and comfort. I am a bit of a bookaholic and have books stacked around me—ones I have read and ones I want to read. Ever since I learned about osmosis, I have thought there ought to be a way of holding a book to your forehead and absorbing it into you—like osmosis. There is never enough time to read.

BEYOND THE AFFAIR

I wrote inspirational quotes in all my journals to "wake me up" and remind me of who I am and where I want to go—like the Twenty-third Psalm. Walking through the valley of the shadow of death describes well my moments of feeling alone and in despair. Remembering my head has been anointed with oil by One who loves me and fills my cup to overflowing gives me pause.

The act of lighting a candle and remembering I am loved by my Creator has in some of my worst moments shifted the gloom and doom into settled assurance. The hard part is remembering to do it.

I managed to stay in incredibly good health during my months of struggle. All of these things were helpful, but I think the biggest healer was my willingness to work as hard and as thoroughly as I knew how—to relearn to love myself, to listen to my heart, and to keep asking for what I wanted. I believed I was in process and trusted that if something hadn't been handled yet, God/Life/the Spirit/a friend/a sunset would point it out to me and I would go back to what needed more work.

42.

Narcissus Is Not Just a Flower

On our way to John's, weaving the car through the back roads to the interstate, I shared with Ken a conclusion I had come to.

"I have decided there may never be any answers to the questions that keep bothering me about the affair, and I think I am at a point where I can let go of wanting the answers."

Ken had been reading the newspaper as we rode along. Tossing the paper into the back seat of the car, he asked, "What questions?"

"Well, for instance, I can't understand why you did all you did, how you could have totally disregarded me. You are such a caring man; I just can't fathom it." Turning onto the ramp of the interstate, I continued, "I think I have been thinking if I knew why you did this, I could fix it so it would never happen again. We haven't talked about this for awhile; do you have any new thoughts?"

There was silence as I threaded the car through the line of cars hurrying along the highway. As I waited for his reply, I noticed the bright red poppies blooming along both sides of the road, their heads bobbing in the wake of the passing cars. I thought, "Flowers give such pleasure, especially along the monotonous interstates."

Ken slowly began to talk. "You know, I think I fell in love with my idealized self through the eyes of Jane. I showed her only me at my best, none of my faults, nothing exposed I didn't want to expose. She thought I was wonderful. She projected back what I wanted her to see. It was me playing the part of

Narcissus, falling in love with my own image. I was totally out of touch with reality and living in a fantasy."

I was fascinated listening to him. "You've never said anything like this."

"It just came to me," he said, sounding a bit amazed. "I was so totally out of touch with reality that I was willing to give up my love for you, our life together, my family, financial security, the job I enjoy, my home, the dogs, everything."

I reached over and touched him. "I can't help saying it, Ken, but it sounds crazy."

"It *was* crazy."

When we arrived at John's office, we were hardly seated when Ken began to tell John the new insight that had come to him in the car on the way to our session.

Then Ken completely stunned me when he said, "I really believe I had a psychotic break."

John sat straight up in his chair, leaned forward, and pointed at Ken, "You bet! It was a psychotic break, plus, add in the addictive power of sex, and you've got exactly what happened. In other words, you were not in touch with reality and would have given up everything—all that you loved and cared for—for sex."

I was amazed and impressed that Ken had put all that together. I also felt relief. Even though in my head I realized it was "our affair" and he was responsible for his behavior, deep in my heart I had convinced myself I was responsible for it all. My head knew that was ridiculous, but my gut said, "You caused this to happen all by your lonesome." I think I was experiencing something similar to what children go through when their parents get a divorce. They convince themselves they are responsible for their parents' decision to eparate. Observers know the child's perception isn't true and just as Ken had aid, it was crazy. It was crazy for him and crazy for me.

John looked at me and said, "Loyd, I hope you are beginning to see the ffair did not mean Ken did not love you and therefore he went elsewhere. He vas not 'out of love' with you. He was caught in a fantasy to the point of ddiction. That is why he was able to say to you that throughout the affair he till loved you."

Right then and there I dropped my belief in my total responsibility like an ld worn-out garment. For now I had a better understanding of what had appened. I also saw how Ken could quickly and completely turn around and lecide to stay and work on our marriage. He still loved me! It was a moment not o be forgotten. I moved farther down my road of healing, and I could feel the ifference inside and out.

43.

The Dreaded Chair

Towards the end of our session, John stood up and walked over to one of the empty chairs in his office. Standing behind it, he asked me, "Do you feel ready to have a conversation with Jane?"

I reluctantly nodded my head, more out of just wanting to get it over with than feeling ready.

Reaching over and patting the seat of the empty chair, John said, "Jane is here and, considering all that has happened, I want you to tell her what kind of relationship you want to have with her now."

Even though I felt nervous, I felt very strong about what I wanted and what I didn't want. The letter I had written her had laid the groundwork for all I had to say.

I knew I wanted my relationship with Jane boiled down to a "professional" relationship, not a "social" relationship. I was willing to be "friendly" but not best buddies. Underneath it all I wanted to get to the place where I could say unequivocally to her that I wished her the best of what life had to offer her. I also wanted to be able to be around her—in her presence—and be solid and absolutely splendiferous in myself. If I was uncomfortable around her, I could always leave, but I had a ways to go to fulfill what I wanted.

Later I discovered one of my resistances to handling my resentment towards Jane and forgiving her. Much to my surprise, I realized I believed to forgive someone meant I would have to become their "best" friend. And if there was one thing I was sure about, it was that I did not want to be her friend, much less her best friend. With this belief I could justify doing nothing, and that's what I did, nothing.

Now I know this may sound odd, but I am sure all this friendship stuff stemmed from my Southern upbringing. Certainly I don't think consciously my mother or father sat me down and taught me I had to be friends with everyone I met, but I know other Southern women who are stuck in this same belief. I think it must have floated into our unconscious on the pungent lemon smell of the magnolias we breathed in every summer.

All my life I have thought I had to be friends with everyone. To maintain good old Southern hospitality, you were required to smile, be nice, and be friendly. And to be friendly was to be friends in my little Southern mind. To have limits, to decide whom you wanted as a friend and whom you did not want was a new concept to me but one I could jolly well get used to.

44.

Comfortable Jeans

Old behavior is hard to let go of. There were days and weeks in which communicating well would have made a big difference in the quality of my life with Ken. But there were occasions when I simply wasn't using all I was learning at John's. It wasn't that I didn't know how; I unconsciously would choose to travel the old road.

Yes, the old road was old and full of potholes, but I traveled it anyway.

Distance and coolness were the modus operandi. I know it is ridiculous to assume I would be or could be a perfect communicator. It would be one thing if I consciously "operated" this way since it would then at least be a choice of behavior I had decided upon. Instead, I would slip back into the familiar cool and distant attire, and it was as comfortable as that old pair of jeans hanging in the back of my closet.

Albert Einstein had a phrase he used when he foresaw the crisis that the splitting of the atom brought on the world. He said, "The unleashed power of the atom has changed everything save our modes of thinking and we thus drift toward unparalleled catastrophe."

That is true in relationships, mine in particular. I would often "drift." Not making the effort to do something differently was often the easiest tack, but Ken and I could never reach the shore together. If I didn't move out of "cool and distant" and continued drifting, I might as well prepare for another catastrophe in my relationship with Ken.

I often shared with Ken, but sometimes I didn't make the effort, choosing to withhold my wants, my complaints, my questions. By withholding, I was not giving Ken the opportunity to share his point of view, his frustrations, his wants. Both of us lose out when either of us fails to say what is going on with us. Sharing the happy things in life is easy, but pain, grief, disappointment, and struggle often get left out. Without both of us freely expressing both the good and the bad, we made it so much easier to feel all sorts of negative emotions, one of which was resentment. I knew better than this and I was disappointed in myself.

45.

A Gift

Forgiveness looms heavy on my heart. My mind intellectualizes the need to be free of grudges, resentments, grievances for the sake of my soul. But my heart hurts and longs to be wrapped in a quilt and rocked into health. Such a struggle.

I recall hearing Archbishop Tutu of South Africa say forgiveness is abandoning the right to revenge or retribution. Whew! Does that ever bring it home to me! He also talked about choosing to forgive as a door of opportunity to make a new beginning. And, bless him, if that weren't enough, he said it doesn't mean you have to become friends.

I was at last ready to deal with letting go of my resentments toward Jane. There was a string of reasons why the time had come. For one, my anger towards her had dissipated—not vanished—but I did not fume at the mere mention of her name. Mostly I sensed the oldness of all my negative feelings, so old I could detect an odor and a weight a bit like having an albatross—a very dead albatross—hanging around my neck and pulling me down.

Even my posture was suffering. I had become aware when I was sitting or driving—even walking at times—my shoulders were curving forward and I bent forward slightly as if I needed to protect myself from some unknown blow. I had also finally understood that forgiveness doesn't automatically translate into friendship. There was nothing, other than me, to stop me from moving forward and just doing it.

I knew better than to go through the process of facing my resentments and letting go of them by myself. I knew how easily I could fool myself into believing I had it all handled. With someone else present it would be harder for me to play the dragonfly and skim along the surface of my complaints. I knew of no one better than June Krug to be with me in the process.

Everyone needs a June in her life!

June and I have known each other for years, often working side by side at workshops as well as taking various workshops together. All of the workshops I've participated in were personal growth workshops, so we know each other very well and have an unspoken commitment to be our true selves when together—no games, no fudging on the truth, just out there in all our glory.

How to describe this special person? Along with her laugh, what stands out for me as "June" is her enormous capacity to love and see the best in me when I can't. She's the quintessential best friend. I could absolutely count on her to be there for me if I needed her and vice versa. Though we lived in different cities, she was as close as my phone and during the last few months we talked often. Ken had had conversations with her as well. He had traveled to her home and had spent time with her doing his own inner work with her help.

I believe June is a mystic. (I can hear her laughing when she reads this.) Like most mystics, it is the last thing she would call herself. Her capacity to intuit what needs to be said or done is one of her gifts. Unafraid to ask you hard questions, she opens the door to deeper levels of thought and feelings untapped on your own. When I am willing to share with her whatever is bothering me, possibilities and choices always abound, and I am no longer stuck in my stuff.

It was natural and comfortable for me to journey to June's and do the work I needed to do to free myself from what had become a heavy burden. The act of deciding to go to her had already made me feel lighter. Why was I so resistant to changing things when doing so made me feel so much better? Humans are a mystery.

137

46.

In Control of the Universe

No sooner had June and I sat down with our cups of tea than I began to talk. Everything on my mind and heart let loose. A dam broke free. The water of words had finally found their way out and begun to crumble the wall of hurt and pain.

We sat in June's living room by the windows overlooking the swimming pool below. The morning sun was shining in, filling us with its warmth. June meditates daily here and has surrounded herself with photographs of her family and important people in her life. Favorite books are stacked on the table among candles and things of meaning to her. It reminded me of my altar at home. It is clearly a holy place, a place of rest, comfort, and connection to that which is at the heart of things.

Holy or not, I was feeling nervous. I felt embarrassed and vulnerable—wide open, exposed, and very tender. Though my mind knew June would not judge me, my insides churned with anxiety as I began my confession.

Yes, it was a confession. I was disclosing, acknowledging all I had resented, all of my grievances and complaints, real or imagined. I wanted to let go of my guilt and forgive Jane not because *she* needed it but because *I* needed it! For the sake of my health and well-being, my soul and I needed to be free of this terrible weight.

"How can I explain the hurt I feel?" I began. "I think the hurt has taken up permanent residence inside of me. I can go through periods of time when I don't feel the hurt and I think, hooray, at last it has disappeared. Then something

138

happens and it is right back in all its ugliness. I don't pretend that everything is 'fine' and I deal with it again, but it has a subterranean life with tunnels going places I don't know are there, only to surface when I least expect it. I am so tired of it!"

June asked the simple question, "Are you willing to let go of the hurt?"

"I keep thinking I have and it returns," I said.

June reached over and gently touched me. "Tell me more about how it feels to be this hurt person. How does it feel to be in your body?"

Amid tears of anguish I moved deeper into the journey. We spent the whole afternoon absorbed in the act of freeing my fingers one by one of all the garbage I had been so intent on holding onto. My list of grievances, complaints, resentments, and grudges towards Jane was filled out more fully. With June's skillful questions we probed deeply underneath it all.

Together we uncovered many of my justifications for holding on to my resentments such as she should be punished, she is a horrible person for doing this to me, she doesn't deserve to be forgiven. I certainly know how she should behave, I was right and she was wrong. The more I could justify myself, the more I could talk ugly about her to my closest friends, get them to agree with me, and I could behave any way I wanted to. After all, I deserved it. I had been wronged, right?

By the time I was finished rattling off all I had been getting out of being so right about everything, Jane was smelling like a rose. I had had no thought of what the effect of behaving this way would have on my body, much less my soul, my heart.

I stopped and looked over at June. She had been intently listening to me with one hand folded softly in her lap and the other resting on her dog, Sissy, who was sound asleep by her side. They were the picture of peace.

I gasped, "I guess I am nothing less than God and in total control of the universe."

It sounds funny now, but at the time I felt sick and shocked at how I had become uglier than any picture I had of Jane.

I had totally misled myself. There was no doubt I had a preference as to how I wanted Jane, or any other woman, to behave toward my husband, but I didn't know how it *should* be—how Jane or anyone else should be. Only God knows how things should be. These things are out of my control. They are as they are.

I hated to admit it, but maybe, just maybe, this needed to happen to Ken and me *and* Jane. Perhaps, it was the only way we could learn a lesson we could not have learned any other way. However, in the midst of hurt and pain I could see the lesson to be learned as a theory, not as a powerful truth.

47.

Coming Home

From the very first night alone in the cabin, weeping and wailing through my pain, I had known that forgiveness would be my saving grace. Forgiveness was always present, wrapping itself around me like a gossamer cloak of possibility. When I wasn't thinking about it, the cloak was light and airy, but when I gave it even a passing thought, it turned into a cloak of iron.

Here in the warmth of June's home cold reality had arrived. I had forgiven Ken. Now it was time to do the dirty deed—forgive Jane. Much has been said about forgiveness. For some, including myself at times, forgiveness has been a "dirty" word or an impossible act. I know better now.

When I was growing up, I believed to forgive someone meant I had to somehow make whatever was done or not done okay with me. I would say, "I forgive you," but deep in my heart, I knew what was done *wasn't* okay with me. Consequently, I went through most of my life believing I hadn't really forgiven anyone. How sad and exhausting to carry around such thoughts for so long. What's more, I was not alone in my belief. I have spent countless hours with others who have the same crippling belief. I have learned much from many.

To forgive Ken was somewhat easier—I love him and live with him. Plus, he shared much that gave me understanding about his actions and willingly worked to change his behavior. I didn't have that with Jane.

It took time even with Ken. I would some days pick up forgiveness like a rock, examine it, and put it back down only to pick it up again. And there were days I would furiously throw the rock as far as I could throw it only to find it resting at my feet waiting patiently. A rock, a cloak, it was always there unavoidable in its presence but easy to ignore.

I said to June, "Ken is my companion, best friend, lover, confidant, my one-man cheerleading squad." As I continued, I was unaware my chin was slowly rising haughtily as I spoke, "Jane is different. She is none of the above. I could probably live my whole life and never see her again. So why bother forgiving her?"

June sat, and I thought, smiled a bit like a Cheshire cat. "Loyd, it is simple and hard to hear, but without forgiving Jane, you will continue to be angry and bitter. And that is true of anyone you refuse to forgive, not just Jane. You know that. Stop a second and get in touch with how you are feeling right now."

I stared blankly at her.

"So how do you feel?" June asked.

What a question. Gazing down at my toes, tears formed in my eyes as I mumbled, "I feel angry, bitter, hopeless, like a little hurt child and my body feels tight." Taking in a breath, I sighed as I crossed my arms across my chest, "Stuck in this stuff."

June stood up. "I am going to get us both a glass of water. While I am gone, take some time to sit with your feelings." She walked toward the kitchen, stopped, and turning she looked back at me and asked, "Do you really want to stay stuck?"

Hearing that question I thought about how I had occasionally heard on the news of mothers forgiving the person who had killed their child. I remembered hearing of a young white American woman who was stoned to death in an African village where she had volunteered to help. The parents not only forgave her killers but took up from where their daughter was brutally cut short and built a school for the village children. Every day as they go to the village, they pass the very spot where their daughter was stoned to death.

How could they do that?

Those parents chose life not death. They let go of their feelings of revenge and redeemed their daughter's death by forgiving her killers—not for the sake of the killers, but for the sake of their own souls. They refused to be bitter, forever unhappy people. I admire and honor their willingness to model forgiveness in the flesh.

If they could, I could. I too choose life. I like the passage from Deuteronomy (Deut. 30: especially verses 15-20, paraphrased)—I can have my life and prosperity or I can have death and disaster. I much prefer life and prosperity. I choose life with Ken unencumbered, free of resentments, and filled with gratitude.

When June came back from the kitchen, I was ready. I had no intention of living my life embittered and angry. It was as simple and as hard as that. To decide to forgive Jane was one of the most freeing actions I have ever experienced.

And so it was done. Quietly and simply I came home to myself.

June and I clicked our water glasses and gave a toast, "To life."

48.

The "C" Word

I'm feeling scared, shaky, vulnerable, wounded, and working hard thinking
am not getting very far because I keep feeling pain. Around and around I go
Somehow I am equating these feelings with not getting anywhere, when in truth
I have made a lot of movement—and as Ken has said, I am courageous
Thinking of meeting with Jane is not easy. She has lied to me, used my
friendship as a way to get to Ken, enjoyed him sexually, planned to be with him
without me, believed Ken was in love with her—in other words—crossed all my
boundaries. I don't trust her behavior. All those are pretty good reasons to feel
uncomfortable. And all seem to be true.

I know my experience at June's was real and I did forgive Jane. I also
realize that I have moments of anger, times when I question if the forgiveness
"took." I keep reminding myself that momentary feelings do not negate all the
work I have done, and I trust I will know when I need to do more work just as
knew it was time to forgive. So live with the feelings, Loyd, and know you are
okay, well-loved by Ken, and have nothing to fear.

The phone rang and it was Debbie. "Hi," she said. "Remember I told you I'd
give you a call if I had some thoughts about why I think the affair has so deeply
hurt you? Not that it isn't hard, but why you seem to be struggling much more
than I would have thought you would?"

I was sitting on the deck taking in the cool morning air. The mountains were
peeking out of a low-lying fog in the valley below, giving it the illusion of a

lake of ice. Sipping my tea and browsing through the morning paper, I had been thinking about the extremes of emotions I feel at times. Earlier this morning I had felt shaky; now enjoying my cup of tea, I felt contented. Listening to Debbie's query, I wasn't so sure I wanted to hear it.

I replied, "Yes, I remember you said you'd call, but I'm not so sure I want to hear what you have to say."

"Well, do you or don't you?" Debbie, ever to the point, said.

"Mmmmm, I'm thinking," I mused out loud. "Yes, I do want to know."

Putting the paper down, I gave her my full attention. Debbie was usually right on the money with her insights, and this one was important to me.

Debbie began to tell me she believed the pain I was experiencing was very different from Ken's or Jane's. Jane was single, uncommitted, no "history" with Ken and could easily pass off the affair as a "fling." Ken was relieved to have it all out in the open, and his pain came primarily from watching my pain. She also reminded me Ken hadn't had the same belief about commitment as I. And that too, she thought, contributed to my pain.

"Commitment" is an earthshaking word with as many meanings as there are people keeping their commitments or avoiding them. Sometimes a lover, by barely whispering anything close to the word "commitment," sends her—and it's usually 'her'—sends her beloved off to the hinterlands never to return. What power this word has. It can bring up fear and trembling, particularly when its meaning is believed to be bonding a relationship together like super glue. This type of bonding guarantees loss of freedom. Other couples see commitment like a wide chasm—the Grand Canyon comes to my mind—impossible to cross. Therefore, they reason, there's no point in trying to commit, and the lack of commitment keeps the relationship from ever feeling secure or owned by them both.

Then there are people like me.

I thought Ken and I were as committed to keeping our marriage vows as any couple could be. To me, commitment equaled being faithful to our vows and each other. However, not so for Ken. He was committed to me. And because he was committed to me, he, on occasion, believed he could do whatever he wanted as long as I didn't find out. We spent hours in therapy uncovering this hidden belief, which was as much a shock to Ken as it was to me. Once the belief was uncovered, we had the golden opportunity to relook at what our vows meant and whether we really wanted to keep them. John reminded us we didn't have to make a decision until September when we would decide whether or not we wanted to recommit to our marriage, including our vows.

Debbie said, "You were kept in the dark. With such a long relationship with Ken and such a strong belief and commitment to the strength of your marriage, you were shaken to the core. Everything was shattered. His commitment didn't match your commitment. You even questioned your own belief in yourself." She paused and said almost apologetically, "I now understand why you have struggled so long and have been in so much pain."

We talked more about how I was feeling and celebrated my journey to June's house. I had felt like a different person since I had stopped carrying around so much resentment. Life certainly wasn't perfect. Ken and I still had much to work through, but I was better, much better.

I asked, "How are *you*, Debbie?"

Such a simple and often meaningless question to ask, but Debbie knew I truly wanted to know and she told me. For the first time in months I had reached out to someone else. When I hung up the phone and picked up the newspaper again, I looked out at the mountains and said loudly enough for the dogs to jump up from sunning themselves, "Yaaahooo! I'm getting better!"

49.

A Change of Mind

Do you know that little niggling voice that sits in the back of your head and reminds you, at first quietly, then raises the volume over time insisting there is something you must do—like it or not? I do, and lately the volume's persistence had caused me to take its challenge seriously.

It started shortly after all this began. First one friend, then another, then another told me in serious tones there would come a time when I might—I held on mightily to the "might"—want to sit down and have a conversation with Jane about how we would relate to one another in the future. Though I would like to have believed we would never see each other again, it wasn't reality. We did have a few shared friends and activities and our towns aren't metropolises, so wanting not to see her at all fit into the same wish as my suppressed desire to walk on water—it wasn't going to happen.

Ken and I had talked off and on about meeting with Jane. When we talked about the various possibilities, enough anxiety was usually produced to close the conversation down pretty quickly. And we would just let it be.

But this evening was different. Ken and I had had a great day working outside pulling weeds in the garden. At this time of the year the land around the cabin is full of lushly blooming mountain laurel, or "ivy" as the old mountain folks call it. Some of the laurels were as tall as small trees with pink blooms calling you to come outside and soak up their beauty. We intentionally have kept much of our land in its natural state, only landscaping around the edges. Even so, it all takes caring hands and we had had a full day.

BEYOND THE AFFAIR

We were puttering around the kitchen putting together some snacks to take out onto the deck and enjoy with our sodas. Ken was in the pantry rooting around for pretzels when I said, "You know, I really would like to talk to Jane. I am ready to stop the imaginary conversations and have a real one." I paused and said, "I can't believe I said that."

I could hear Ken laughing inside the pantry. Holding a bag of his favorite brand of pretzels, he turned around and said to me, "It's amazing. Here I have been thinking the same thing and the next thing I know you are saying what I am thinking."

Picking up his glass, he gave me a little kiss on my neck as he walked by. "Let's go out on the deck and talk some more."

The deck faces toward the western mountains. Ridge after ridge ripple forward until they reach the horizon of the high curving rim of the Blue Ridge Mountains off in the distance. In the early summer the breeze is soft and cool, blowing the leaves in the trees like instruments in a well-rehearsed symphony. On evenings like this with the sun beginning to alert us to a stunning end to the day, the view is breathtaking and feelings of gratitude well up and spill out with words like "Isn't this incredible?" and "Aren't we fortunate?" and "We are so blessed."

We looked at each other and smiled. "I love you," he said. "And I love you too," I replied.

50.

The Invitation

Phone calls had been made, and nervous conversations had taken place. Ken and I invited Jane to meet with us on a Friday evening at Debbie's house. Jane very graciously accepted. I had moments of total incredulity—could we really be doing this? Then I would switch to moments of clarity—the place where I knew my heart and my mind were connected and I was at one with myself.

We suggested Jane was welcome to bring someone to be with her—a supporter, a friend. We had asked Debbie to be that person for us. I particularly wanted Debbie to be willing, and she was, to have the courage to jump into the conversation and stop it if I blew it and fell into anger or blaming Jane for all that had happened.

The drive to Debbie's that Friday evening was quiet. Ken and I were both engrossed in our own thoughts. As we drove around the last curve into the parking lot I could see Jane's car wasn't parked by Debbie's house and I felt a wave of relief. I would have time to get centered, take some deep breaths, and arrange myself—literally—before Jane and her friend arrived.

Debbie had the garage door open. Ken and I walked around her car and up the inside stairs which opened into the living room. I couldn't help but see the metaphor of moving through the basement up into the *living* room. Even the images of moving from dark to light were clearly present and didn't escape running through my mind as encouraging signs.

As I hugged Debbie I realized I was only a breath away from shaking from head to toe.

BEYOND THE AFFAIR

She held on to me and reading my thoughts said, "You are fine—take some deep breaths and let go and go ahead and shake if you want to."

I laughed self-consciously.

Walking around the room, I did as she had said and began to feel a bit calmer—but only a bit. I reminded myself of Ken when he was in college and was preparing to run the mile or cross-country race. He would stretch up and down, shake his hands furiously, jump up and down first on one foot then the other, and do his best to work the tension out of his body.

Ken fixed tea for all of us. He seemed much calmer than me. We found our spots on the sofa, settled in, and waited for whatever was to come next.

51.

The Meeting

The arrival of Jane and her friend was announced by their footsteps sounding on the wooden stairs as they came up the garage stairway into the room. Ken and I exchanged momentary panicked looks. Then he whispered, "All shall be well," and leaned over and put his hand over mine.

Automatic pleasantries were exchanged. Tea was poured and seats were found amid the nervous tension that pervaded the room.

Ken, thank heavens, began.

It took time as we all worked through levels of sharing, but when we got into the depths of what we wanted one another to know, the room changed as well as the people in it. Even the lighting looked different—everything was soft as though bathed in candlelight. There is meager vocabulary to describe the space we all created there in Debbie's home. The best I can say is it was sacred. Ken said it was an experience of the kingdom of heaven—how we are with one another when we are intentionally wanting the best for each other.

Once we had begun, I was completely at ease. I had moved into another state of being. The prayers of many were with us that night. Could that be how we did what we did? Being there, listening, saying what I had to say was effortless. At times I was amazed at myself and surprised hearing my words. I could feel myself move away from "me" in detached, loving observation of all that was going on. I had truly passed through the valley of the shadow of death. I was being my true, authentic self, and it was awesome.

BEYOND THE AFFAIR

I don't know how Jane felt. She was full of tears. At one point near the end of our time together, I asked her if there was anything more she wanted to say to me. She said, "Well, you know I am sorry. Do you think you can forgive me?"

I said, "I have forgiven you—you have that. And, no, I didn't know if you were sorry. It is important for me to hear you say it, thank you. You look like you need a hug." Who said that? *I* said that?

Jane nodded her head. No one could have told me I would ever have managed holding Jane with ease. At least not in this lifetime. But it was as natural as holding one of my own children.

Miracles never cease.

52.

Looking Back

I know you may have guessed what happened in September, but I will tell you anyway.

The month of September arrived with no particular fanfare, no stellar fireworks signifying this was the month of "mutual decision." One ordinary evening Ken and I were sitting together on the sofa talking about Annie and her new beau, Tim, and wondering out loud if he was "the one." Ken turned to me and simply said, "You know, Loyd, you are 'the one' for me."

"Ahh," I said feeling touched by his sweetness.

"Shall we make our commitment to stay together? Maybe restate our vows?" he asked.

I looked at him and knew I wanted to be with him forever just as I always had. "Yes," I said. "Let's do it!"

Jumping up to get his Prayer Book, he called out to me, "We need a ring."

I called back, "Look in my jewelry box."

When he arrived with book and ring in hand, we cuddled up on the sofa and through tears of joy recommitted our life together by reading our vows to each other—one more time. Ken slipped on my finger a twenty dollar ring I had found in a funky store while visiting New Orleans with Annie. It could have been Tiffany's finest for all it meant to me.

BEYOND THE AFFAIR

Four years later looking back at that hard time in our life, we have amazingly expanded and grown beyond our affair. I know I will never take our relationship for granted again nor will I not appreciate the pain of process.

I stand taller, surer of myself and humbler, much humbler. Lessons I have learned get relearned—sometimes daily. Life together is rich, fun, warm, and full of love and affection. And yes, at times we struggle, disagree—the Southern euphemism for "fight"—forget to communicate, occasionally keep secrets, but not for long.

I have done more work on forgiveness of Ken, of Jane, and of myself. I forget sometimes that forgiveness is a process of many levels, not a "done deal" that is complete once and for all. I picture it as a spiral going upward. The more I am willing to explore the level that has appeared, the less painful bumping into old feelings of anger and hurt threaten me. Sometimes it is a slow go and other times a breeze. I am not afraid. Always, always grace appears welcoming me home. Even though the book is finished the process goes on, and I feel the progress deep in my soul.

There is a big difference with who we are and how we are with one another. Kindness comes to my mind—kindness and a respect that come from long talks and many hours of the hard labor it takes to get to the bottom of upsets and ultimately forgive one another. There is no freedom like the freedom of having nothing that separates you from the one you love. There is a depth of love so deep it can't be measured. We nearly lost a treasure. "Time heals all wounds," they say. I say, "Time heals all wounds if you want it to and you work very hard at it."

Ken's story, which he tells eloquently, is a part of my story and he shares it with you now.

Afterword by Ken Kinnett

As I write, I am sitting on our deck on a cool Saturday afternoon in May under a sunny "Carolina blue" sky. Looking west across twenty miles of Blue Ridge Mountains, my eyes are resting on a blanket of spring-green foliage. Loyd is away on the local garden tour. As I soak up the beauty of this corner of God's world, I am thinking, "How could I ever have conceived of not living with Loyd the rest of my life and living in this place?"

Willie Nelson on the CD player is singing, "She's a good lovin' woman in love with a good timin' man." I realize now is an appropriate time to write my part of Loyd's book of hope. It has been in the back of my mind to do for weeks. Tuesday Carolyn, a friend in Atlanta, admonished me, "It is time for you to write your part."

At the moment I have the treat of the company of Clio and Buster. Buster is our third Jack Russell terrier—the one we picked out as a pup four months after the sharp pain and sadness had eased after Dickens's death from a brain tumor. Even with the dogs' presence, I respond to Willie's song with an emptiness in my stomach—loneliness. Next comes the poignancy and sadness of recalling that February four years ago when Loyd shocked me with what felt like a bucket of cold water on my face and a fist in my stomach. Guilt clinched my heart as she asked something like, "You're having an affair, aren't you?"

I don't recall much of the two days that followed. I do remember the difficulty of being with Loyd as she poured out first her dismay over realizing I was having an affair, and then her anger over having been betrayed by me. I do remember I didn't want to tell Loyd the name of the woman involved. I caved in to try to appease her anger. I clearly remember I was pretty well convinced I was ready to leave Loyd and fly to Jane.

BEYOND THE AFFAIR

Loyd has written beautifully and in detail of the pain, as well as the relief that came after months of dealing with our situation with friends, our therapist, and, most importantly, with each other. As I look back from the perspective of a healed relationship, the more appropriate song, which I played earlier today, is Louis Armstrong singing, "It's a wonderful world."

My story had started months earlier with another woman in Atlanta, who had been a friend years ago. I had come close to consummating an affair with her, but she was not willing to go past heavy petting. To meet her in Atlanta meant a four-hour drive. After our first partial love-making night, we missed meeting each other twice at designated places. I gave up trying after a few more phone calls. I decided having an affair closer to home would be easier. That is when I made a romantic advance towards Jane and she returned the favor.

I had had amorous thoughts and feelings for Jane during the previous summer. At that time I made a sexual comment to her and thought I sensed her being responsive. In late fall I followed my intuition with a willful decision to approach her. Once I had made the decision to make a romantic move towards her, I felt my heart race. Isn't that always true with young love, or better, new love? (Neither of us was exactly young.) I drove to her place unannounced and knocked on her door holding a red rose. Once inside her living room we fell into a long embrace and kiss. I felt attracted to her not only for her looks but also because she is an intelligent woman with a bright personality. She was warm, affectionate, caring, and as eager as I to make love. She filled a place in my life that I had not experienced with Loyd in many months. We had grown apart, or surely I had grown apart from Loyd, from a lack of communicating fully and from taking her for granted. The mutual passion Jane and I experienced those three months was something I had not had with Loyd for—how long? I'm not sure now.

This doesn't mean Loyd was "at fault," whatever that means. It is about how I was perceiving our relationship and responding by withdrawing rather than looking for ways to mend it. I could have let Loyd know what was going on with me but decided it would take too much effort. I convinced myself that I deserved to have more sexual pleasure in my life with someone else. Instead of finding ways to create it with Loyd, I decided to look elsewhere. It would be easier, I reasoned, than doing the work of restoring what I thought was missing in our relationship.

Whenever I could find an excuse, I concocted some story that would cover a trip to spend a few hours with Jane. I also made many lengthy calls to her from my car phone. Once together, we were both so hungry physically for each other that we rarely got around to having long talks and really getting to know one another. She remarked about this a couple of times, but we headed for the bed, except on two occasions—a drive back from Atlanta and a picnic one afternoon at a pull-off on a mountain road.

Looking back from the perspective of four years and a marriage that is better than ever, I can see past my "other brain's" urges—what some women call men's "small brain." I had become entranced with my idealized self that Jane reflected back to me. The Greek myth of Narcissus and Echo had come alive. I later came to see with the help of John Hoover, our therapist in Knoxville, that I was engaged in addictive behavior with Jane, not love. I, who had been an alcoholism counselor, was blind to addiction's signs: being secretive, binging on my "drug" of choice, and denying I was doing anything detrimental to my health, in this case my mental, emotional, and moral health.

During the months that followed Loyd's discovery of my affair, a number of factors contributed to our staying together. Loyd's and my decisions to stay were primary—not just to stay in the relationship until we worked through the trauma, but to stay together in our home and bed. Another factor was courage. I feel awkward saying I was courageous, but I was and Loyd was. There was also the support of friends who loved us both and John Hoover, our skillful therapist. Undergirding it all was the gift of grace, that quality and power which comes from outside oneself to enable goodness to prevail.

The pivotal moment for my decision to stay in our marriage came the day after Loyd confronted me with her discovery of my unfaithfulness. I was looking for Dickens, our Jack Russell terrier who had run off hours before. Loyd describes that incident, but it was so powerful for me that I am including it too. After unsuccessful drives down country roads to find Dickens, I set out on foot and headed down the path to the Indian Cave, one of his favorite places. It is a powerful place. I have gone there to meditate and have had answers come to me that did not come from meditating anywhere else. As I rounded the corner of the path where the ground in front of the cave comes into view, I saw Dickens. I grabbed a small sapling on the left side of the path—something I'd never done before. It did not move but was as steady as an iron bar. Something within me would not allow me to let go. Within seconds I realized I would not let go of my marriage either. I decided to stay in our marriage and return to Loyd if she would have me.

In the next moment, the critic in my mind said, "You don't mean it. You're just deciding that to make it easy on yourself." I knew I did mean it. I recalled what my mentor in sales training, Scott Roy, said at a sales meeting one morning at the cancer insurance company for which I worked in the early '90s, "David Dean, who taught me the art of sales, said you can change your mind in a split second." I don't recall the context, but he was probably talking about changing negative thinking. At any rate that memory reinforced my decision, one that would eventually lead to a new wholeness of life for me and us.

Once I made my decision to stay in our marriage, I was determined to take whatever Loyd confronted me with—doubts, fears, rage, distrust, tears, and questions—anything she needed to express. I knew the offense was mine, I was responsible for it, and I knew the road to restoration led through hearing and living with all of Loyd's anguish. It was not easy hearing how much she suffered as a result of my infidelity, but I knew if healing was to come, it would take my being fully present with her as her hurt poured out. Thanks to hundreds of hours of personal growth training, I had excellent listening tools as did Loyd. The ability to listen played a large part in our staying together while we worked through the trauma.

At times, the pain Loyd was feeling was not anything I wanted to be around. It emanated from her with an energy that penetrated my inner being and felt as sharp as razors in my gut. I had intentionally, selfishly, and consciously begun the affair. I did it strictly for my own pleasure, knowing Loyd would not suspect anything. I knew how much she trusted me. Yes, I used her trust against her in order to pleasure myself. I didn't try to justify it in my own mind except by the self-absorbed thought, "I deserve to have this pleasure." Fully aware that I had consciously chosen to be unfaithful to Loyd, I just as consciously took responsibility for my actions and chose to embark on my part of rebuilding our marriage.

It is a testament to the character of our three children that, first, they would come and be with me as well as with Loyd within a week after the discovery and, second, that they were willing to hear me out with open hearts. This, when their hearts must have been heavy over their dad's actions—their own father! What comfort to have Brian, David, and Annie love us and stand by us as we worked this through, not knowing the outcome, but trusting their folks to find the right answers. I was also, like Loyd, comforted by the presence of our dogs. To stroke them and be aware of their unconditional love relieved my anxiety. It helped especially to have Dickens or Clio in my lap while listening to Loyd describe her suffering.

The twice weekly trips to see John Hoover in Knoxville and hours on I-40 in our Toyota Camry, proved to be some of the most critical times for me. Sitting next to each other in the front seat for two and a half hours each way gave me time simply to *be with* Loyd. We talked of our anxiety and fears on the way over. On the way back home, we reviewed what we had experienced at John's caring hands and from his challenging questions. We rode in silence at times. It was comfortable silence. I never felt coldness or anger from Loyd.

I believe the months between February and September, the month we made our final decision to stay together, were easier for me than for Loyd. Once I had made my decision to stay, the fear of discovery, the false exhilaration of "getting away with it," my narcissism and selfishness which had been diminishing my true self, and my guilt were all pretty much over for me. A strange aspect of the human condition, isn't it, that most of my pain was over as Loyd's was beginning and intensifying?

I am grateful every day that she was willing to stay with me while she went through the trauma, first of facing me with her knowledge I was having an affair and then through the intensifying pain that followed for her. I am grateful daily that she would not even entertain the thought of sending me away, and I am supremely grateful for the quality of the relationship we have now. Perhaps it was necessary that all of this came about to wake me up to the preciousness of our relationship and what it takes for a marriage—or any other long-term relationship—to keep its aliveness. One agreement we made is not to keep secrets. Loyd had had this commitment all along and now I made it mine also.

A grace-filled moment occurred recently that confirmed our relationship is solid. I saw Jane at a social gathering. We had a couple of brief, friendly conversations. I felt no emotional charge. It was like having a casual conversation with any other acquaintance.

I hope the story of my breaking the relationship and our going through the process of healing it speaks to you. Our marriage is more life-giving and satisfying than ever—emotionally, sexually, affectionally, mentally, and spiritually. Our relationship is virtually stress-free. When stress does occur, usually from a grievance or resentment, we handle it and let go of it. There are no secrets on my part any more. It is true freedom.

The following poem was a gift to me from Loyd, "With renewed love in celebration of our 39th anniversary." It tells the cave story in a way that moved me and I want to share it with you.

Have hope. It is yours for the taking—our gift to you.

Poem:
The Cave And The Cave Revisited

The cave waits patiently.
It is old and has had many visitors,
Among them the Cherokees,
Who hid sustenance and magic
   within its walls.

Small boys, lovers, curiosity seekers
Wanting to find a piece of what was
Come looking for something and
Go away touched, strangely satisfied, moved
   by the cave.

You sense it when you approach it.
The ground is hallowed.
Unseen Spirits guard the entrance
Watching and waiting to serve.

Years ago the cave was sealed by a white man's fear.
No matter, the cave remains,
Quiet as in sleep but a source of energy.
Once a place for ceremonies and healing,
   its ancient spells still felt.

A place of refuge, solace, nurturing,
Healing felt deep within one's own cave.
Why else are many called, pulled
To make a pilgrimage to what now looks
   to be a pile of rocks?

BEYOND THE AFFAIR

Yes, solace still found here—comfort.
One cave recognizing another cave.
And the Spirits stand, offering to serve
Their gifts of presence and blessing.

*****

Another white man approaches
The entrance to the old cave,
Also frightened, troubled,
Anguishing over a heavy decision
   not decided.

Drawn to that spot
In search of a beloved missing dog or
Was it his missing beloved,
His own lost Self, his Cave,
   his knowing.

Looking up from where he stood
Bracing himself with the help of a tree
(the staff left by a wandering shepherd?),
He was met by the guardian Spirits.

In their hands they brought him gifts,
Gifts from the cave.
The gift of courage, the gift of a remembered love,
The gift of wisdom, the gift of forgiveness, the
   gift of his lost heart.

Once more the Spirits gave their blessing
And—he decided.

An Invitation:
Kinnett Partners, L.L.C.

As a result of the work Loyd and Ken went through in their process of recreating their relationship, they designed a relationship skills workshop, Loving You Loving Me. In this workshop couples learn from Loyd and Ken the skills they have learned. You are welcomed into their mountain home, Mariposa (Spanish for "butterfly"), where you can get away from the busy world and focus on your relationship—simply and intimately—and transform it into a butterfly.

The Kinnetts often work with one couple at a time as well as with groups. The magic of the workshop comes from working with material you know best, your own life experience. Within that powerful frame of reference, you build new partnering skills. With the help of hands-on support from Loyd and Ken, you will learn the use of simple, powerful skills to make a difference in all your relationships for the rest of your life.

Credits: Ch. 32: ©1981 Drake & Tyler, The ANGEL® Cards Book
Ch. 44: Otto Nathan and Heinz Norden, eds., Einstein on Peace, New York: Avnel Books, 1981 ed., Page 376

Visit *www.kinnett.com* for information on the workshops that grew out of this experience and *www.takeheartcoaching.com* to learn how you can be in a coaching relationship with Loyd to move beyond an affair or other betrayal in your life.

CPSIA information can be obtained at www.ICGtesting.com
Printed in the USA
BVOW081146260812

298776BV00001B/6/A